BEHIND THE SCENES IN
HORSE RACING
• CHARLIE HURT •

BEHIND THE SCENES IN
HORSE RACING
• CHARLIE HURT •

PARTRIDGE PRESS

LONDON · NEW YORK · TORONTO · SYDNEY · AUCKLAND

TRANSWORLD PUBLISHERS LTD
61-63 Uxbridge Road, London W5 5SA

TRANSWORLD PUBLISHERS (AUSTRALIA) PTY LTD
15-23 Helles Avenue, Moorebank, NSW 2170

TRANSWORLD PUBLISHERS (NZ) LTD
3 William Pickering Drive
Albany, Auckland

Published 1992 by Partridge Press
a division of Transworld Publishers Ltd
Copyright © Morgan Samuel Editions 1992

The right of Charlie Hurt to be identified
as author of this work has been asserted in accordance
with section 77 and 78 of the Copyright Designs and
Patents Act 1988.

A catalogue record for this book is available from the British Library

ISBN 185 225 1808

Typeset in Candida at 10pt on 12pt by Blackjacks, London.

Separated, printed and bound by Toppan Printing Co (HK) Ltd.

CONTENTS

FOREWORD BY JEFFREY BERNARD

SPECULATORS MAY DECIDE to gamble on a yearling judged on its breeding, but there are hundreds of hours of hard work behind the scenes to be considered, too. Preparing for the first race is an intricate and skillful task involving many people. You could call them the backroom boys of the turf, although the trainer himself is not exactly backward in coming forward. Clive Brittain, who has co-operated so kindly with Charlie Hurt to enable him to produce this excellent book, is one of the old-school trainers, a sort of throwback to the days when trainers were described by gentlemen owners as being 'mere grooms'. Clive Brittain is not 'mere' anything.

The stable lads in a large yard based in a racing centre like Newmarket can look pretty daunting at first sight. Nowadays some lads (and lasses) can even be seen to be smoking cigarettes when they ride out to the gallops and the clothes they wear, jeans and wellies, would make the likes of Fred Archer and the Honourable George Lambton turn in their graves. And vets and farriers must be extremely brave men since it is more dangerous to walk around the back end of a horse than it is to back it.

But what is extraordinary about everybody involved in racing, from the people who load into slanting stalls to the great trainers themselves, is that they invariably fall in love with their charges.

It is extraordinary, too, that so much expertise and hard work can go into the rather trivial business of seeing whether one horse can go faster than another. And it is remarkable that this trivial pursuit can attract such an enormous cross-section of the population. The sport of kings is also, remember, the sport of layabouts, tramps and the ne'er-do-well after a quick buck.

In the earliest days of racing, from the Regency to Victorian times, especially Victorian times, most jockeys were recruited from the ranks of undernourished working-class boys from all over Britain, and particularly the north. Being a jockey was originally a Dickensian occupation. So many chimney sweeps and Oliver Twists, of which the lucky few who got to the top of the tree always boasted that they had been apprenticed in rat-infested barns. It was recorded that the unsuccessful of the profession ended up dying in those same rat-infested barns.

The last apprentice I spoke to, one afternoon at Newbury races, offered me a lift home in his red Ferrari and I noticed that he was wearing a Rolex Oyster.

All this for kicking home a horse for possibly as little as five furlongs. Mind you, the whole business is extremely dangerous physically, and financially when an owner is anxious about his or her self-esteem. One can always insult an

owner's child, but it is forbidden to criticise the horse.

The excitement of racing extends and expands the television in a sitting room to a summer's day of being on the course at Ascot, York, Chantilly, or New-bury. For me hundreds of attendances at the races have amounted to hundreds of al fresco cocktail parties. On the other hand, there is nothing quite like the buzz to be got by watching race horses do fast work on the gallops on a spring or summer dawn. The noise of the hooves slamming into the turf, the jangling of bits and bridles, the bellowing of lungs, particularly when they snort out feather-like plumes of air on a cold morning, is beautiful.

I have never believed that race horses are particularly clever. The majority of British people believe horses to be as clever as Roy Rogers' Trigger. In fact, I believe horses to be exceptionally, on occasions, sadly tractable. An animal that can actually enjoy running in the Ascot Gold Cup would have to be a masochist.

The author, Charlie Hurt, edited my attempt at writing a book about racing. This took the form of spending ten days with him in Norfolk pubs. I also at one time dictated an entire racing book to him in the Coach and Horses Pub in Soho. I doubt that either of us have recovered from those experiences, but at least he still loves racing and it shows.

Jeffrey Bernard

INTRODUCTION

THERE have been many books about horse racing over the years. They have come in all shapes and sizes and have covered every aspect of the sport, from the sometimes entertaining but often trite memoirs of jockeys and gamblers, to learned treatises on the fascinating but inexact science of breeding. Recently the trend has been either for beautifully packaged overall guides to the sport, lavishly illustrated with scores of artistic photographs, or for highly impressive but necessarily rather dry books of statistics made possible by the onset of the computer age.

There are many photographs and not a few statistics in *Behind the Scenes in Horse Racing*, but similarities to previous publications end there. For *Behind the Scenes* is an attempt to do just what its title implies – go behind the scenes in horseracing and explore those areas of the sport which are often skimped or ignored by more general books but which are of great interest to the racing enthusiast.

What really goes on at the trainer's yard? What is the daily routine? How is the horse entered for races; which races and why? And what are the responsibilities of the travelling head lad, the Clerk of the Course, the stipendiary Steward? What goes into producing the day at the races that so many people enjoy yet mostly take for granted?

Behind the Scenes in Horse Racing deals with the nuts and bolts of horseracing and tries to answer many of the questions that the enthusiast would ask if he found himself in the right situation to do so. For this purpose we have enlisted the help of three establishments in particular: Clive Brittain's Carlburg Stables, and Lord Howard de Walden's Plantation Stud at Newmarket, and Newmarket racecourse, courtesy of the Clerk of the Course, Nick Lees.

All three establishments are, of course, successful and well-known, and were carefully chosen as examples of first-class working operations. Clive Brittain, Lord Howard de Walden and Nick Lees and all their respective staffs, have been

► *Clive Brittain watches the second lot at Newmarket.*

Lord Howard de Walden's Slip Anchor, winner of the greatest test of all, the Epsom Derby, seen at home at Plantation Stud, Newmarket.
▼

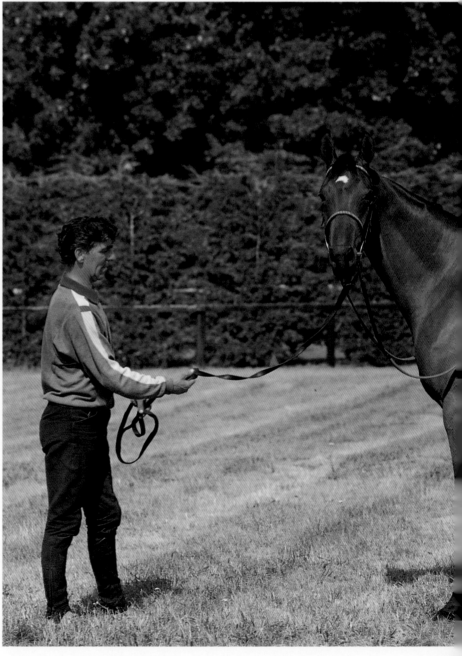

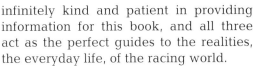

◄ *Transcript at Clive Brittain's yard.*

► *Transcript at Newbury on 12th June, 1991, coming alongside Lester Piggott's mount.*

infinitely kind and patient in providing information for this book, and all three act as the perfect guides to the realities, the everyday life, of the racing world.

Behind the Scenes in Horse Racing also focuses on a particular horse from Clive Brittain's yard. Nobody would claim that Transcript is a world beater, and that is exactly why we chose her. We wanted to concentrate on an average racehorse and see how its career progressed, from foaling to the racecourse. It would be nice, we thought, if she won a race, but it was not essential, and we certainly weren't relying on it. By examining the experiences of this horse we hoped

to learn about the experiences of the average racehorse. For it is the average racehorse, not the Dancing Brave or Nashwan, that makes up the vast majority of the many thousands in training each year.

And the average racehorse is what this book is all about. Here you will find no stirring tales of superheroes, equine or human, no paeans of praise to top trainers, jockeys or owners, but a factual and accurate account of what actually goes on in the racing year – what goes right and what goes wrong. I have attempted to transmit my fascination and enthusiasm for the greatest of sports to the many other enthusiasts all over the world, for this book is not limited to British racing, but it also investigates the similarities and differences of racing in other countries around the globe, in particular Japan, Italy, Germany, France, Australia and the United States of America.

Finally, my thanks to Trevor Jones and George Selwyn, whose superb photographs accompany the text.

THE WORLD OF HORSE RACING

THEN AND NOW

NOBODY knows when the first organized horse racing took place, though there has been no lack of scholarly research into the subject. The answer must be: shortly after man first learned to ride, when the first argument about which horse was the fastest was settled by practical means. It is a safe bet that horse racing took place in some form or other in many equestrian-based societies of the ancient world, and there is certainly evidence to suggest that the Romans indulged in the sport. They are believed to have staged race meetings at York and Chester, for example, during their occupation of Britain.

And it is to Britain, or more precisely England, that we must turn first in this brief history, for it was there that the basis of modern horse racing was laid. It is not in dispute that there was racing at places such as York, Pontefract, Salisbury, Doncaster and Epsom in the 16th and 17th centuries, while it was Charles II who put Newmarket on the map as a horse-racing centre whose influence and importance grew swiftly during the next five reigns, as did the sport as a whole.

During this seminal period the foundations of the Thoroughbred racehorse were also put down, with the importation to England of many stallions from Arabia, Turkey and Barbary (present-day Algeria and Morocco), most famously the Darley Arabian, the Godolphin Arabian and the Byerley Turk. All modern Thoroughbreds descend in the male line from these three. Their progeny, Matchem, Eclipse, Herod and Highflyer became the four great sires of the second half of the 18th century, a time when racing underwent such profound changes that it transmuted itself into something recognizably similar to modern-day racing.

It is from that time that the "Racing Calendar" can be dated, recording as it did the day-to-day history of British

Statue of the great Eclipse, after whom the Eclipse Stakes is named, at Newmarket. Eclipse's exploits gave rise to the saying "Eclipse first, the rest nowhere." ▼

▶ *Christopher Haines is Chief Executive of the Jockey Club. The post has only recently been created in an attempt to give the long established, self-electing body a more business-like image in the harsh modern world. Yet many problems for the Jockey Club and racing as a whole lie ahead.*

ECLIPSE
1764

racing, and from then can be traced the racing of two-year-olds, the institution of handicap racing and, most significant of all, the beginning of the Classic races. All major racing countries in the world have, in their own time, followed suit.

It was during the 19th century that the sport was honed and refined under the auspices of the Jockey Club, which grew greatly in power throughout this period, and in particular under the administration, guidance and presidency of the great Admiral Rous. Both the racing and breeding sides of the sport had made such immense progress and improvements in the 200 years since the time of Charles II that the publication of Rous' book *On the Laws and Practice of Horse Racing* in 1850 quite neatly marks a watershed. Many of the elements of modern-day racing were by then in place and the changes of the last 140 years have in the main been changes of emphasis, detail, style and technological advances rather than of substance.

Indeed, a comparison between modern racing and that of its Golden Age is remarkable not so much for how greatly racing has changed but for how little. In social terms things are very different, of course, but that is more a reflection of how society, rather than racing, has developed. By the "Golden Age" I refer to the closing decades of the 19th century, an era of great horses like St. Simon, Ormonde and Persimmon, and one dominated by arguably the greatest jockey of all time, the superlative Fred Archer, winner of 2,748 races, including 21 Classics, and 13 times the champion

▲
"They're off!" at Kempton Park, one of two courses tucked away in the London suburbs, the other being Sandown Park. In a sprint race a good start is essential.

▼
The amazing Lester Piggott, perhaps the greatest jockey of all time, made a sensational return to the saddle in 1990 after years in retirement and a prison sentence, with a win in the Breeders Cup series in the United States for his old ally Vincent O'Brien. Racecourse attendances swelled as the crowds crammed through the turnstiles to see the legendary "longfellow" in action again, but some professionals dreaded the possibility of seeing him being beaten by a younger man in a tight finish.

jockey in his 17 years in the saddle before the fateful day when he blew his brains out at Newmarket in 1886 at the age of 29. Reading accounts of those days it is astonishing how closely they parallel the modern British racing season. Many of the races and race meetings are still the same, with the same crescendoes and high spots during the year.

There have, of course, been many changes, of greater and lesser significance: the introduction of professional stewards' secretaries; the advent of starting stalls; technical improvements such as photo-finishes, patrol cameras, and public address systems; the establishment of the Tote (the Horseracing Totalisator Board) in 1929 and the Horserace Betting Levy Board in 1960; and the legalization of off-course betting, to name but a few. Modern-day racing is an altogether more efficient and more streamlined affair, though many would argue that it is still not efficient enough.

THE PATTERN

PERHAPS the most important development in modern horse racing, certainly in terms of international racing, has been the introduction of the Pattern. The Pattern is a largely successful attempt to view the season's racing as a whole and to make sure that the best horses have a series of valuable races to suit their varying needs in terms of age and distance. The idea originated with the Jockey Club in the 1960s. It soon spread to Europe, and is now accepted by most major horse-racing countries, including the United States.

▶ *One of the most thrilling sights in European racing in recent years has been that of Steve Cauthen, the great American jockey, often leading his rivals from pillar to post with superb displays of split timing. Here he brings Reference Point home at Doncaster to win the St. Leger.*

▼ *Sunday Silence beats Easy Goer in the Breeders Cup Classic of 1989.*

Pattern races are divided into three groups: Group One for championship races, including Classic races, in which horses meet on weight-for-age terms with no penalties or allowances; Group Two for races just below championship standard in which there may be penalties and/or allowances; Group Three for races of mainly domestic interest, including trials for the Classic races, which complete the series of tests for the best horses.

From the International Pattern has sprung the International Classifications – a system of rating horses by weight, 64kg (140lb) being the norm for a horse capable of dominating its contemporaries. It is now possible to compare the best horses of different countries, even if, as is likely, they have never met on the racecourse. However, with continuing improvements in transport, and an increasing understanding and willingness among trainers to travel their horses, the likelihood of,

▲
A fine Italian champion beats a fine British one as Tony Bin just holds Mtoto in the 1988 Prix de l'Arc de Triomphe at Longchamp.

◄
Quest for Fame, in the hands of the champion jockey Pat Eddery, wins the Epsom Derby in 1990 to give first-season trainer Roger Charlton a fairy tale beginning to his career.

▼
Sanglamore takes Le Prix du Jockey Club, the French Derby, in the famous colours of Khalid Abdullah, to give trainer, owner and jockey a famous double. A few days before the same team had won the Epsom Derby with Quest for Fame.

for example, an Epsom Derby winner meeting the victor of the Kentucky Derby increases every year, and this is the single most exciting aspect for world racing as the 21st century approaches. The French-trained Azari's spectacular success in the USA in 1991 proves that travel should be no handicap.

Level-weight races and handicap races

Broadly speaking, races fall into two main categories: level-weight races and handicaps.

Level-weight races are events in which the runners compete against each other carrying the same or similar weights. They range in class from the Derby itself down to the most humble maiden race (a "maiden" being a horse that has never won a race). Various allowances and penalties, written into the conditions of the race, may or may not alter the weights carried by certain entries.

Handicaps are races in which the entrants carry different weights, computed by the Jockey Club handicapper, according to their varying abilities. In theory, the horses in a perfect handicap race should pass the winning post strung out across the course in a straight line, something that in practice, needless to say, never happens.

All ages of horse are eligible for both types of race. Three-year-olds and above can race over any distance between 5 furlongs and just over 2¾ miles, depending on their preferences. There are restrictions for two-year-olds, however. They may race over 5 furlongs from the beginning of the season, over 6 furlongs from mid-May, over 7 furlongs from June, and as far as a 1¼ mile from August.

BRITISH HORSE RACING

FEW PEOPLE would deny that during the 1980s Britain saw some of the best racing in the world. It was certainly comparable to the best that the United States had to offer and exceeded that offered by the French who, with their far higher levels of prize money, were pre-eminent in Europe as recently as the 1970s. The sole reason for Britain's current excellence has been, since the 1980s, the continuing involvement with British racing on a massive scale of the Arabs, in particular the Al Maktoum family of Dubai and Khalid Abdullah of Saudi Arabia. They maintain studs and stables in various countries, but they have made Britain their base, partly because of their liking for the tempo and variety of the British racing season, partly because of their respect for the professionals of British racing, and partly because British racing retains a certain mystique, largely due to its unrivalled historical heritage. This last point alone explains why the Epsom Derby, despite slipping down the scale of worldwide races in financial terms, is still the race which everybody wants to win.

The Derby is the most important race in Britain, the number one among the Group One races. However, very few owners ever have a horse worthy of being entered, yet alone winning, a Group race, and Group races make up only a small proportion, about 100, of the

▲
A race develops on the all-weather track at Lingfield. All-weather racing is a new element in the British racing scene, welcomed by many, including the bookmakers, but scorned by others.

▼
Owner and breeder Lord Derby. It was his ancestor who, on the flip of a coin, gave his name to the greatest horse race in the world.

3,000 staged each year. There are some 10,000 owners registered with the Jockey Club in the average year, though many will not own horses that are actually in training. Approximately 7,500 will race each season, chasing total prize money of some £25 million. Only one horse in four, however, actually manages to win a race, however lowly, while over half of horses entered fail to be placed in any of their attempts at success.

The horses in training are spread among over 400 trainers with licenses to operate on the flat. Of these, over 150 will fail to win a single race in any given season, while others, at the top of the tree, will win well over a 100 races each. They have a choice of 36 courses to which they can send their charges (there are two at Newmarket), from Hamilton Park in the north to Brighton in the south, from Ayr in the west of Scotland to Yarmouth on the Norfolk coast. They present an almost bewildering range of variations and idiosyncrasies that would not be countenanced in many self-respecting racing nations, from the tight, left-handed 1 mile circuit of Chester to the vast expanses of Newmarket Heath, from the magnificently flat and fair circuit of York to the thrilling switchback of Epsom or the unique figure-of-eight of Windsor.

In a typical year some 200 jockeys and apprentice jockeys win at least one race. Many jockeys are attached to particular

▲
One of the most delightful and more idiosyncratic racecourses in Britain is Chester where each May a huge and enthusiastic crowd witnesses a thrilling programme of races round its tight turns.

◄
The most powerful owner in the world is Sheikh Mohammed. He has won nearly everything there is to win, but the ultimate prize, the Epsom Derby, still eludes him. Here he is seen in conversation with one of his many trainers, the Newmarket-based Italian Luca Cumani, who himself landed the Derby with Khayasi in 1988.

◄
One horse with more claims than most to be European Horse of the 1980s was the thrilling Nashwan. Here he spread-eagles the 1989 Derby field in the hands of Willie Carson and the colours of Hamdan Al-Maktoum to bring a glint into the eye of his wheelchair-bound veteran trainer Major Dick Hern, doyen of the British professionals.

stables, while others prefer, or are forced, to ride freelance. As in any profession, talents vary from individual to individual, from the lesser lights, thankful for a few rides a season, to the great international riders of our time, such as Willie Carson, Steve Cauthen and Pat Eddery.

It is often said, disparagingly, that modern flat racing is no longer a sport but an industry and there is a large amount of truth in this. Some 100,000 people are employed in racing and its allied professions, while the pressures at the top mean that all too often a potential champion horse is hustled off to stud without being given the chance to prove himself or, more to the point, not prove himself, on the racetrack. Nevertheless, it is often aficionados of jump racing who take the flat to task, and many of the charges are unfair.

It is quite certain that when Hamdan Al-Maktoum wins the Derby he does not see it entirely in terms of fiscal reward. Indeed, such a suggestion would constitute a slur on a thoroughly sporting owner. It is even more certain that when the average owner of an average leg of an average racehorse wins £666 as his or her share from a handicap seller at Pontefract, it is not just the money that induces him to jump up and down in the winners' enclosure, grin like a clown and kiss everyone in sight, from trainer to gateman. Could it possibly also be the nature of the sport?

◀ The handsome trophy for the Arlington Million, one of the most sought after in American racing.

◀ American trainer Wayne Lucas has won almost everything there is to win on his home territory and, in true American style, just keeps on winning. On horseback, however, he looks marginally less stylish than some of his jockeys.

▼ Racing under the big skies and palms on the Gulfstream course, Florida.

AMERICA

Argentina

Argentina has a Pattern and Classic programme based on Europe's, and the emphasis is on stamina rather than speed. Its horses have distinguished themselves among North American rivals, and Argentinian strains have made their mark in Europe too.

However, in recent years political and economic problems have not helped the Argentinian racing and breeding industries, and a tendency towards the boosting of speed at the expense of stamina is unlikely to be the answer. Moreover, there is a theory that the breed is coarsened after three or four generations on Argentinian pasture, and that the declining imports of decent stallions and mares, vital to keep up standards, could have serious consequences.

North America

The USA and Canada have the largest Thoroughbred population in the world, and the two countries tend to be grouped together for the purposes of statistics. The USA has a long, chequered, but influential history as a breeding and racing nation, and can now claim to be the most important country in the world for the breeding of top-class racehorses, particularly in the area known as the Kentucky Bluegrass. Canada, on the other hand, has only come to the forefront in recent years, though the Canadian-bred Northern Dancer is certainly the single most important sire of post-war years.

Racing in the USA varies from state to state and it must be said that the majority of the many tens of thousands of races

staged each year are matters of very little consequence, often run on dirt tracks over very short distances at breakneck pace by horses trained at the course and often under the influence of drugs such as Lasix and Butazolidin (of the major racing states only New York bans their use). Unlike in Europe, racing continues all the year round, and a meeting at a particular course can last for weeks or even months (hence the necessity for dirt tracks).

The system of Graded racing, the North American equivalent of Europe's Pattern, includes the American Triple Crown and the Breeders Cup series of races, held at major courses such as Hollywood Park, Aqueduct, Santa Anita, Churchill Downs, Pimlico and Belmont.

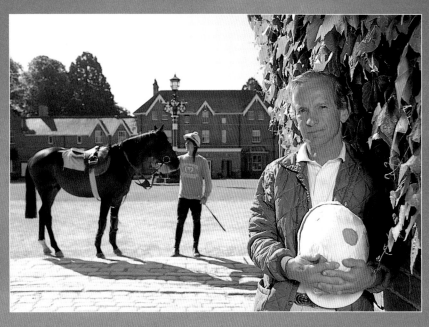

▲
Bill Shoemaker, "The Shoe", won more races than any other jockey in the world up to his recent retirement. Here he poses at Robert Sangster's lavish Manton complex, then in the hands of trainer Barry Hills. Shoemaker narrowly failed to win the Epsom Derby for Sangster and Hills when narrowly beaten by Shirley Heights in 1978.

◄
Shortly after the off on the dirt at Churchill Downs, Kentucky, home of the Kentucky Derby, the first leg in the American Triple Crown.

In Graded racing the accent is on excellence at the middle distance, and, in contrast to European racing, horses racing at Graded level do so without a break between their two-year-old and three-year-old seasons, competing from the September of the first season through to the June of the second.

Canada has its own Triple Crown, restricted to Canadian-bred horses, and also stages two important international events, the Rothmans International and the E.P. Taylor Stakes, both run at Woodbine.

Although the 1980s saw more and more competition between Europe and North America, and increasing international competition is certainly where the future of world horse racing lies, there are many problems still to be ironed out, in particular the differences between racing on turf and dirt, and the unfair advantages, or perhaps ultimately the disadvantages, for American horses which are allowed to race under medication.

EUROPE

France

France vies with Britain for dominance over European racing and shares a great deal in common, having reformed itself in the second half of this century, putting a premium more and more on speed at the expense of its hitherto favoured stamina. Some would say that with the recent reduction in length of the once glorious long-distance Grand Prix de Paris to a mere 1 mile 2 furlongs, the French are taking things a little too far. They are less keen than the British on two-year-old races, which are largely restricted on the top courses until May. French racing is more soundly and generously financed than British racing, and prize money is correspondingly better. Bookmakers have been banned since 1891. The sport is masterfully overseen by the Société d'Encouragement under the leadership of the formidable Jean Romanet, but just as the French were historically slow, compared to England, to organize the racing of horses, so the French people are less smitten with the game than their counterparts across the Channel, and weekday racing can be a soulless and sparsely-attended affair.

French racing is very much more centralized than in Britain. While there are provincial tracks, the vast majority of racing is carried out at the cluster of tracks around Paris, headed by Longchamp, the main exception to this being during the month of August, when the entire racing community decamps to the Norman resort of Deauville.

▲ *Horses pass the stands at Maison Lafitte, one of the cluster of French tracks to hold top-class racing within easy distance of Paris.*

▶ *One of the most successful French trainers in recent years has been François Boutin, who, quick to appreciate the growing international flavour of horse-racing, has made sure that his overseas raiders are always to be feared. Here he holds court to the press.*

▼ *One of the more unusual spectacles in European racing is the Grand Prix St. Moritz, on ground that would not be appreciated at Royal Ascot.*

Germany

Despite establishing a racing tradition in the 19th century based on the English one, Germany subsequently fell behind France and Italy for various reasons and was not surprisingly in a very poor state by the end of World War II. Since then great strides have been taken, and their very best horses are now considered world standard. The German racing industry is smaller than the British (with only 14 courses, for example), but it is based on similar lines, being overseen by the Direktorium Fur Vollblutzucht Und Rennen. One main difference is that two-year-olds are not allowed to run before 1st June.

Italy

Italy's place on the world horse-racing map owes more than a little to the genius of one man, Federico Tesio, who died in 1954. He bred and raced about a dozen top-class horses, including the world-beaters Nearco and Ribot (though sadly he did not live to see the latter win the Prix de l'Arc de Triomphe twice) and he almost single-handedly elevated the status and reputation of Italian racing. Since his death, Italy has failed to maintain its momentum, though it is still capable of producing the occasional world-class animal. Its structure and season follow the usual European Pattern, though staying races are generally favoured at the expense of sprints.

Republic of Ireland

The smallness of Ireland in terms of area and of human and Thoroughbred population belies its importance as a centre for racing and, in particular, for breeding. Both are intelligently supported by the government of the country and nurtured by a natural love and understanding of the horse by the Irish people, while the racing tradition in Ireland is as old as any in Europe.

In recent years Irish horses have won many of the top European races, the stable of Vincent O'Brien having been particularly feared, and have returned triumphant from several trans-Atlantic crossings. An increase in sponsorship has meant that the Irish Classic programme is now on a par with that in Britain and France, and the season and structure of Ireland's racing is very similar.

▲
Top British horse-racing journalist and television presenter Brough Scott, a former amateur jump-jockey, conducts an interview with the owners of Tony Bin, winner of Le Prix de L'Arc de Triomphe.

▼
Every lover of horse-racing should try to get to Laytown on the Republic of Ireland's east coast where the events take place on the sand. The prize money may be less than at Longchamp, but the atmosphere is unbeatable.

The great Irish trainer Vincent O'Brien has dominated the principal races of Europe for three decades and, though he is less in evidence now he is in the autumn of his years, he is still able to work his magic on the big occasion, as his success with Royal Academy in the 1990 Breeders Cup series demonstrated. Royal Academy was ridden that day by Lester Piggott, who had just returned from a five-year retirement, and it was with him that O'Brien scored many of his victories. For the record, O'Brien has won the 1,000 Guineas, the 2,000 Guineas (four times), the Derby (six times), the Oaks (twice), the St. Leger (three times), the Irish 1,000 Guineas (three times), the Irish 2,000 Guineas (four times), the Irish Derby (four times), the Irish Oaks (four times), the Irish St. Leger (eight times), Le Prix du Jockey-Club and Le Prix de L'Arc de Triomphe (twice).

REST OF THE WORLD

Australia

Despite the unsuitability of much of its terrain and climate, and its small population, Australia is the second largest producer of Thoroughbreds in the world after North America. Australian racing is similar to British in many respects. It has a properly defined season, two-year-old racing is encouraged, and staying races are still the backbone of the sport. Two major differences are that geldings are allowed to take their place in the Classics, and non-Thoroughbred horses make up about one-third of the racing population.

Another is that Australians are commendably less soft on their horses than the British, who rush potential champions off to stud almost as soon as their hooves have touched a racecourse. In Australia a champion is a true champion having proved him or herself after two or three seasons on the track. One of the reasons why this is feasible is that stud values have not reached the astronomical proportions of Europe and America, so it is worthwhile to keep a horse racing.

The very best Australian racehorses are comparable with the top class of other major racing nations, though in the

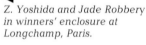

Horses after exercise at Lindsay Park, Adelaide, Australia.

lower divisions there are many very moderate animals taking part in a mass of race meetings of little account. So there is a sharp division in Australian racing between the quality racing, involving a small number of horses, professionals and racetracks, and the rest.

The sport is well organized and soundly financed, and the Australians have a genuine love and enthusiasm for their racing which goes as far as any other factor in explaining its increasing success.

Japan

Japan lies behind only three other countries – the United States, Australia and Argentina – in terms of the quantity of Thoroughbreds produced each year, but has so far been unable to produce a racehorse that has proved itself in the top class among foreign company abroad. Japan's late entry into the Thoroughbred breeding market (at the end of the 19th century) and the devastation caused by World War II are the main reasons for her comparative slowness to produce quality. As Japan marches forward in almost all areas, however, it is likely to be only a question of time before this is rectified.

In recent years many top stallions have been imported from the European market, but a lingering protectionism is slowing down Japan's claim to be considered as a major factor in world racing. Their 10 major courses stage some 3000 races a year, of which only about 15 per cent are open to foreign competition, while their Pattern races, just under a 100 in all, are

Z. Yoshida and Jade Robbery in winners' enclosure at Longchamp, Paris.

unacceptable in the international system. In general, staying races for three-year-olds and older horses are favoured at the expense of events for sprinters and speedy two-year-olds.

Like most things Japanese, the racing industry is very efficient, and while there is no doubting its increasing success, some might disparage its comparative lack of colour and its centralization.

New Zealand

New Zealand is the Ireland of the southern hemisphere and breeds a large number of Thoroughbreds, specializing in tough, middle-distance types for the home and Australian markets. The legendary Phar Lap, foaled in 1926, is perhaps the best known of all New Zealand-bred horses, and since then several of their horses have competed honourably at the highest world class level.

Until the 1970s, New Zealand racing was largely a law unto itself, but it has been rationalized since then. A Classic series has been created on the European model, and now, with the introduction of Graded races corresponding to Pattern races elsewhere, and the first running of a $NZ 1 million race in 1989, the country has taken its rightful place among the leaders of world horse racing.

Hong Kong

Nobody would pretend that the quality of racing in Hong Kong could match that of the major countries, and some would go as far as to dub it mere "animated gambling", but few would deny that it is as exciting as any in the world, and more exciting than most. In the 20 years since it has had a professional sport, Hong Kong has attracted many of the world's top jockeys to perform in front of its packed stands at both the long-established Happy Valley track, and at the new Sha Tin track, one of the wonders of the racing world, built on land reclaimed from the sea.

▲ *An extraordinary backdrop for an evening meeting at Hong Kong's Happy Valley racecourse. The racing may not be world class, but the excitement is electric.*

◄ *Happy Valley, Hong Kong. They race by daylight, too.*

South Africa

South Africa has long been an important country for Thoroughbred breeding and racing in terms of quantity, but not quality. Although it has bred a few top-class animals, it is generally thought that the emphasis on speed at the expense of stamina has limited the success, in world terms, of its racing. Paradoxically, as in Australia, it is the big staying handicap that is the particular favourite of the South African racegoer. Another problem has been the regionalized nature of the racing, resulting in the staging of four different Derbys in one season. The competitive nature of much of the racing in South Africa, however, coupled with its popularity as a spectator sport, has meant that high standards are often achieved within these limitations, and the South African multiple champion jockey, Michael Roberts, is currently one of the most sought-after on the British and European circuit.

FINDING A HORSE

THE DREAM of every small owner is to spend next to nothing on a two-year-old, mop up three or four of the better juvenile races, watch it coast to victory as a three-year-old in the Derby, make the trip to Paris to shout it home in a thrilling, hard-fought victory in the Arc de Triomphe and finally syndicate it to stand at stud for several millions. Extraordinary things happen in the racing world, and you will hear any number of stories about bargain-basement equine stars and multi-million pound flops, but the truth is that on the whole the more you spend the better you get.

Breeding a horse

There are many different ways of acquiring a racehorse. Perhaps the most basic, but also the most difficult way is to breed it yourself. To achieve this you need, at the very least, a mare, a paddock, a stable and access to a stallion, and certainly for the more fortunate type of owner there can be no more satisfying process (*see pages 38-9*). For most people, however, it is a question of buying an animal, and it goes without saying that the road to success is full of pitfalls.

Buying at the sales

The most obvious place to buy a racehorse is at the sales. Sales of yearlings are staged in all the main Thoroughbred breeding countries of the world. The most famous – and expensive – are at Keeneland in the United States, at Newmarket in England, at Deauville in France and at Kill in Ireland. Sales deal with animals of different grades. Some, like the Keeneland Select in Kentucky, or the Tattersalls Highflyer at Newmarket, only deal with the most blue-blooded and potentially expensive animals. Others are less exclusive. All have a certain excitement in common, and a day at the sales is thoroughly recommended for anyone interested in the world of horse racing.

Not least among the attractions of the sales is the opportunity of studying racing people, a breed apart, in their own habitat. Some gatherings of like-minded professionals occasionally discuss other matters than their own subject. Among racing people there is only one topic, and one alone – horses.

▼ *Doncaster Sales. The horses are walked up and down for potential owners. The talk is all conformation and breeding. Hope fills the air.*

Buying through a trainer

Another way to acquire a horse is to buy one from a trainer. Often a trainer will bid for a horse at the sales with a view to passing it on to one of his owners. It is fairly safe to assume that the trainer must have seen some potential in the horse for him to buy it in the first place. There is, therefore, a chance that the horse in question has, within its own limitations, reasonable prospects of picking up a race. Most sensible trainers will usually have an eye to the future, and if they want to keep their owners they will sell them a horse with which they are likely to have some fun.

▲ *Doncaster Sales. The end result of many months' hard work for stud staff will shortly be led into the sales ring, only to be led away into different hands after a possibly glorious, or perhaps ignominious, minute or two in the limelight.*

WHAT TO LOO[

Most buyers and sellers of quality racehorses would agree that a decent pedigree is essential. But they would also concur that, however impressively a pedigree might read, the animal in question has to please as an individual. Some people have an eye for a horse, some do not. Among the points to look for in a horse's conformation are: big ears and eyes, often taken as a sign of genuineness; plenty of space about the nostrils and a well-made jaw; a good, long neck; clean, straight limbs and a good walk and action – legs should be free of heat, lumps and bumps; a decent depth of girth allowing ample room for heart and lungs; feet of the right size in proportion to the rest of the body.

Part-ownership

There is often the possibility of buying merely a leg, or less, in a horse; that is, buying into a partnership of up to 12 persons. Other people prefer to lease, while recent years have seen a huge growth in the popularity of racing clubs, where for a greater or lesser outlay an individual can share in the ownership of one or more horses safe in the knowledge that if things go wrong he or she cannot be called upon for more resources after the initial payment.

Selling and claiming races

The intrepid would-be owner can always resort to yet another method of finding a horse. Throughout the season most racecourses stage selling and claiming races, the most lowly form of event in the calendar, though of course their quality varies widely. After a selling race, the winner is put up for auction in the winners' enclosure. It cannot be bought for less than the added prize money for the race. Very often it will attract no bid at all and thus be led out unsold. Very often, if there are bids, the owner or trainer will fight very hard to retain their horse. Other horses in a selling race may also be claimed at a price stipulated in the race conditions.

A claiming race is a marginally superior type of event. All horses may be claimed for a certain price, depending on what weight they carried in the race.

▼
After the selling race at Bath. The winner, Bobs Ballad, is sold for 4,700 guineas.

Claims are submitted to the Clerk of the Course after the race, and the best claim will secure the animal. The obvious snag to buying a horse from a seller or a claimer is that the very fact that the horse is running in such an event means that it probably has very limited ability (though, as in all racing matters, there are startling exceptions to the rule). The other, less obvious snag is that certain trainers and owners, especially those with yards full of moderate selling platers, do not take kindly to being bid up to high prices to retain or fail to retain, their horses. Understandably, they take even less kindly to having them claimed.

R IN A HORSE

Perhaps as good a method of rating the appearance of a horse as any other is that devised by the late Joe Thomas of Windfields Farm in America. Allowing a maximum of 100 marks, he divided up the points of a horse into different values as follows:

- 25 marks for overall appearance (size, presence, condition, bone etc.).

- 10 marks for the top line – head, neck, throat line, shoulder, withers, back, croup and tail.

- 35 marks for the forelegs.

- 15 marks for the hind legs.

- 15 marks for the gait.

A VISIT TO THE SALES

THE OLD-ESTABLISHED firm of Tattersalls hold the sales at Newmarket at their large and impressive Park Paddocks complex just behind the High Street. The area is divided up into exercise grounds, lunging rings, horse walks, car and horsebox parks, examination rings, paddocks, restaurants, canteens and stabling for some 700 horses. At the heart of it all is the sale-ring itself.

In sales lasting three days there might be close to 900 horses, or "lots", put under the hammer. Most of the potential buyers will have some idea of which lot or lots they are interested in before the start of the sale, having studied the catalogue in advance. They are at liberty to inspect any or all of the horses in or out of their boxes and to have them walked and trotted before they are led into the sale-ring. One maxim should always be borne in mind by the wise: *caveat emptor*, let the buyer beware. Even the most scrupulous and honest of vendors is unlikely to advertise a horse's bad points, and the less scrupulous have various methods of concealing them.

Deauville: the stallion Lead On Time out for a stroll.

THE SALE CATALOGUE

All around the ring throughout the sale, heads will be buried in the catalogue, which will have its own distinct style of presentation, depending on the company. A system of "black type" is used for horses' names. To take Tattersalls' own example, it works as follows:

HAMMER – *winner of a European Pattern Race, a Foreign Graded Stakes Race, a Listed Race or a Major American Stakes Race.*

Hammer – *a placed horse in the above races.*

HAMMER – a winner of a flat race.

Hammer– *a winner of a National Hunt race or a non-winner.*

Hammer – a winner of a National Hunt Pattern race.

Hammer– *a placed horse in a National Hunt Pattern race.*

The catalogue also gives the horse's pedigree for the last three generations. It then lists the exploits, both on the racecourse and in the paddocks, of the horse's dam (mother), second dam (grandmother) and third dam (great grandmother). But while all the offspring, good, bad and indifferent, of the dam will usually be listed, only the winning offspring of the second and third dams will be mentioned. Thus, while the catalogue speaks only the truth, that truth errs on the side of the economical.

With the recent advances in computerised handicapping, and the now possible link between classifications of horses in many of the major horse racing countries of the world, the system of black type is effectively outdated and would be better replaced by one which included the international classification of each horse mentioned. This would allow the reader of the catalogue to see at a glance exactly which of the horses was best in racing terms.

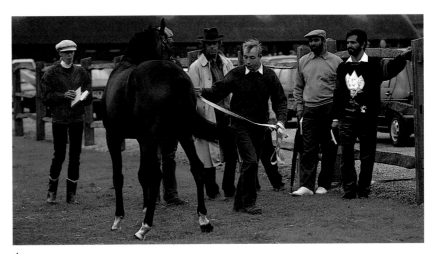

▲
No owner has more buying power than Sheikh Mohammed (right), and no trainer has had better results in the last 20 years than Henry Cecil (in hat and coat), whose astonishing strike rate, allied to the size and quality of his stable, has forced the record books to be rewritten on various occasions. They are seen together here at Tattersalls Sales.

◄
The sales. Clive Brittain inspects Lot 126, a colt by Natroun.

◄
Clive Brittain's yard: a Robellino colt sold by Mary James and bought by the British Bloodstock Association (BBA) for the nice round figure of 100,000 guineas.

►
Tattersalls sales: Prince Khalid Abdullah (centre), one of the biggest spenders on bloodstock in the world, passes the time of day. One of his most successful trainers, Guy Harwood, is behind him to his left, summing up the qualities, or lack of them, of a possible purchase.

►
Perhaps the greatest trainer of them all, the legendary Vincent O'Brien (wearing mackintosh and hat), seen at Tattersalls Sales.

Viewing

Shortly before a horse's entry into the ring it will be led into the nearby upper sale paddock where it will join half a dozen other animals waiting their turn. It is common for one or more of them to be called out at the last moment to the nearby examination box by a prospective buyer naturally wishing to inspect it at close quarters.

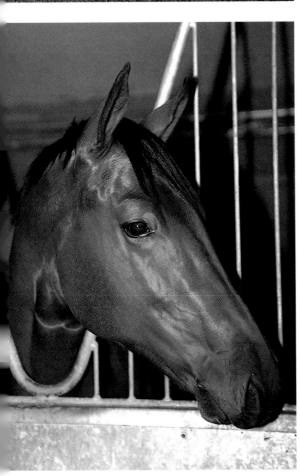

THE AUCTION RING

THE HORSE is led into the ring. If it is a beautifully bred animal expected to reach a high price there will be a buzz of excitement. More likely there will be a general air of nonchalance except among a couple of potential bidders. The auctioneer will announce the lot: "Number 582, a nice-looking bay filly by Elegant Air out of Teye and closely related to some good winners. Who'll start me at ten thousand guineas? Ten thousand guineas? Now come on gentlemen, we haven't got all morning. Do I hear five

Tattersalls: the auctioneer in full persuasive cry.

Tattersalls: a horse is led round the ring, just passing the auctioneer's rostrum. The bidding is on. The illuminated number board reflects its worth at that precise second.

thousand guineas?...Thank you, sir. ...Starting at five thousand guineas, then. ...Six thousand...."

And so the bidding commences. Every auctioneer has his own style, some quiet and self-effacing, some sharp and humorous, some aggressive and bullying. Some, like David Pim, "Pim's Number One", have become minor celebrities in their own right. What all will know, along with the horse's vendor, is the closely guarded secret of the reserve price, and if the horse doesn't reach that price, it will be led out unsold.

Facing the auctioneer round the ring will be various assistants, scanning the crowd for bids. And alongside him on the rostrum there will be "spotters" to assist him further in his task. Just before you begin to tire of a particular auctioneer's style he will imperceptibly slip away to

Present at every sales worth attending is Tony Morris, who writes on breeding for the Racing Post, and is generally acknowledged to be one of the world's foremost experts on the subject. He can usually be seen sitting quietly at his word processor, not far from the auctioneer's rostrum.

be replaced by another with a different face, voice and approach. So the momentum, the atmosphere of hustle, bustle and hurry, is kept at a high pitch, and the prospective buyers, many of whom would no doubt prefer a more leisurely pace, are kept up to the mark.

Occasionally a very famous trainer or owner will walk into the ring, creating a slight stir among the rest of the crowd. He and his entourage will take up their position as the object of their desire is led in. They may remain aloof as the bidding goes through the early stages and only enter the fray when the prices reach a realistic level. More often than not, the opposition will melt away as the great man raises his hand, knowing that it has met its match. And after only a brief appearance, the colt or filly secured for his stable, the trainer or owner will walk back into the open air, taking with him that little aura of excitement.

It is impossible not to feel sorry for the grooms. Some of them will have been with their charges since their foaling days and must feel a pang of real sorrow as they see them sold to a new owner and led away to a new life.

▲
Tattersalls: one of the best sales teams in the business.

▼
Lot 74, by Green Desert, goes through the ring.

Buying through a third party

Most small or inexperienced owners prefer to let their trainer or bloodstock agent bid for them, having told them that they are prepared to go up to a certain price. Either way, they will be charged 5 per cent of the sale price as commission. If the owner wants to bid himself, and he or she is unknown to the sales company, he will have to establish his credentials and credit beforehand.

Buying a racehorse is fraught with danger, and anyone who tells you differently is either ignorant or untrustworthy. While the chances of buying a good 'un, one that might actually win a race, are small, it is the sad fact that the chances of eventually re-selling at a profit are also insignificant, or 18% according to figures produced by the Racehorse Owners' Association, and they are in the best position to know.

Nevertheless, and despite all the logical reasons why not to, owners persist in their thousands in buying and racing horses and most of them, though they can usually recite a long list of trials, tribulations and grievances, will tell you that they gain immense pleasure in doing so. The truth is that the thrill of seeing your colours pass the post in front, even on the humblest of occasions, is a thrill that, for the racing fiend, surpasses all others, and people will go to extraordinary lengths to achieve it. In these days of syndicates and part-ownership it is possible to own a leg in a moderate animal without necessarily having to remortgage the house, and it is a fact that a group of friends, all sharing the triumphs and disappointments, can have just as much fun as the single owner.

BREEDING

BLOODLINES

ALL THOROUGHBREDS are descended in the male line from three horses imported to England from the east at the end of the 16th and beginning of the 17th centuries: the Godolphin Arabian, the Darley Arabian and the Byerley Turk. The Curwen Bay Barb is also is represented in many pedigrees.

It is the male line that has traditionally been considered of most influence in the breeding of racehorses and, despite modern trends, this is still largely the case, partly because a successful stallion might, during a lifetime, get as many as 500 foals compared to a successful broodmare's 8, partly because of an old-fashioned and unproven bias. Nevertheless, it is common for a fashionably-bred animal to be the product of a stallion who was raced successfully at the highest possible level, and a mare who may never have won a race or even been put into training.

Modern-day breeding is more than ever a game of chance. Only 5 per cent of stallions can properly be considered successful at stud, while less than 25 per cent of their progeny in training will ever win a race, however lowly. Fashions in modern breeding change with the wind, and it is now common for stallions to be hyped and oversold only to fall from grace a couple of years later before being given a proper chance to prove their worth. The great Canadian-bred Northern Dancer (descended from the Darley Arabian) has been the supreme stallion of recent years, and his progeny are continuing the good work.

The revolution in prices put into motion by Robert Sangster in the 1970s and perpetuated by the Maktoums in the 1980s has forced out most of the smaller and many of the larger owner-breeders. Only massive breeding empires, like that of the Aga Khan, based on outstanding Thoroughbred families, can hope to compete. American stock now dominates the world, and the prospects for Europe are bleak. They will surely remain so while prize-money stays proportionately low.

The breeding of racehorses has been described by the eminent breeder (of Brigadier Gerard), John Hislop, as an 'inexact science'. By breeding the best to

the best there is always the possibility of producing the best, but it always remains merely a possibility. The full brother of a great racehorse can be incapable of win-

▼
The Byerley Turk was named after a Captain Byerley who rode one during the King William III Wars in Ireland.

ning a race. In general, very good horses produce less good offspring, while less good horses are sometimes capable of producing great ones.

ALLEGED
Bay Colt 1974

Hoist The Flag (b.1968)	Tom Rolfe	Ribot
		Pocahontas
	Wavy Navy	War Admiral
		Triomphe
Princess Pout (b.1966)	Prince John	Princequillo
		Not Afraid
	Determined Lady	Determine
		Tumbling

BRED: JUNE McKNIGHT (USA). WINNER OF 9 OUT OF 10 RACES INCLUDING: Prix de L'Arc de Triomphe x2, Great Voltigeur Stakes, Gallinule Stakes, Royal Whip Stakes.

ALYDAR
Chestnut Colt 1975

Raise A Native (ch. 1961)	Native Dancer	Polynesian
		Geisha
	Raise You	Case Ace
		Lady Glory
Sweet Tooth (b. 1965)	On-and-On	Nasrullah
		Two Lea
	Plum Cake	Ponder
		Real Delight

BRED: CALUMET FARMS (USA). WINNER OF 14 OUT OF 26 RACES INCLUDING: Sapling Stakes, Champagne Stakes, Flamingo Stakes, Florida Derby, Blue Grass Stakes, Travers Stakes.

ARDROSS
Bay Colt 1976

Run The Gantlet (b.1968)	Tom Rolfe	Ribot
		Pocahontas
	First Feather	First Landing
		Quill
Le Melody (b.1971)	Levmoss	Le Levanstell
		Feemoss
	Arctic Melody	Arctic Slave
		Bell Bird

BRED: PADDY PRENDERGAST (IRE). WINNER OF 14 OUT OF 24 RACES INCLUDING: Ascot Gold Cup, Prix Royal Oak, Yorkshire Cup, Goodwood Cup, Geoffrey Freer Stakes.

BRIGADIER GERARD
Bay Colt 1968

Queen's Hussar (b.1960)	March Past	Petition
		Marcelette
	Jojo	Vilmorin
		Fairy Jane
La Paiva (ch.1956)	Prince Chevalier	Prince Rose
		Chevalerie
	Brazen Molly	Horus
		Molly Adare

BRED: JOHN HISLOP (UK). WINNER OF 17 OUT OF 18 RACES INCLUDING: Middle Park Stakes, 2000 Guineas Stakes, Sussex Stakes, Champion Stakes, Eclipse Stakes.

DANCING BRAVE
Bay Colt 1983

Lyphard (b.1969)	Northern Dancer	Nearctic
		Natalma
	Goofed	Court Martial
		Barra
Navajo Princess (b.1974)	Drone	Sir Gaylord
		Cap and Bells
	Olmec	Pago Pago
		Chocolate Beau

BRED: GLEN OAK FARM (USA). WINNER OF 8 OUT OF 10 STARTS INCLUDING: Craven Stakes, 2000 Guineas Stakes, Eclipse Stakes, King George VI and Queen Elizabeth Stakes, Select Stakes, Prix de L'Arc de Triomphe.

FORLI
Chestnut Colt 1963

Aristophanes (ch.1948)	Hyperion	Gainsborough
		Selene
	Commotion	Mieuxce
		Riot
Trevisa (ch.1951)	Advocate	Fair Trial
		Guiding Star
	Venetia	Foxglove
		Dogaresa

BRED: HARAS OJO DE AGUA (ARG). WINNER OF 9 OUT OF 10 STARTS INCLUDING: Polla de Potrillas, Gran Premio Jockey Club, Gran Premio Nacional, Gran Premio Carlos Pellegrini.

KRIS
Chestnut Colt 1976

Sharpen Up (ch.1969)	Atan	Native Dancer
		Mixed Marriage
	Rocchetta	Rockefella
		Chambioes
Doubly Sure (b.1971)	Reliance	Tantieme
		Relance
	Soft Angels	Crepello
		Sweet Angel

BRED: LORD HOWARD DE WALDEN (UK). WINNER OF 14 OUT OF 16 RACES INCLUDING: Sussex Stakes, St. James's Palace Stakes, Goodwood Mile, Queen Elizabeth II Stakes, Lockinge Stakes.

PEDIGREES

THE FOUR vital qualities which breeders are always searching for are speed, stamina, temperament and soundness. It is thought that certain families of Thoroughbreds produce their best off-spring when crossed with each other. This is called a "nick". It is remarkable how often the same names occur in the pedigrees of many top-class horses, as can be seen from these pedigrees of highly successful colts of the recent past.

The breeding of racehorses is more than ever big business. The days of long-established studs where the breeder quietly nurtured the well-being of offspring of tried-and-tested family lines have largely gone. Now the international bloodstock agent is an important cog in the machine, and trainers and owners at the big sales, about to part with small fortunes, are usually surrounded by a coterie of experts.

▲ *Alleged at Doncaster, 1977.*

▲ *Brigadier Gerard wins the Eclipse Stakes, Sandown, 1972.*

Kris wins the ▲ *Waterford Crystal Mile, Ascot, 1979.*

▲ *The Minstrel after winning the 1977 Derby.*

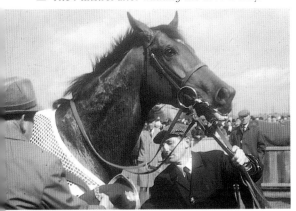

▲ *The incomparable Nijinsky.*

▲ *Sea Bird II winning the 1965 Derby.*

▲ *Shirley Heights winning the 1978 Derby.*

MILL REEF
Bay Colt 1968

Never Bend	Nasrullah	Nearco	
(b.1960)		Mumtaz Begum	
	Lalun	Djeddah	
		Be Faithful	
Milan Mill	Princequillo	Prince Rose	
(b.1962)		Cosquilla	
	Virginia Water	Count Fleet	
		Red Ray	

BRED: PAUL MELLON (USA). WINNER OF 12 OUT OF 14 RACES INCLUDING: Dewhurst Stakes, Derby Stakes, Eclipse Stakes, King George VI and Queen Elizabeth Stakes, Prix de L'Arc de Triomphe, Prix Ganay, Coronation Cup.

THE MINSTREL
Chestnut Colt 1974

Northern Dancer	Nearctic	Nearco	
(b. 1961)		Lady Angela	
	Natalma	Native Dancer	
		Almahmoud	
Fleur	Victoria Park	Chop Chop	
(b. 1964)		Victoriana	
	Flaming Page	Bull Page	
		Flaring Top	

BRED: EDWARD TAYLOR (CAN.). WINNER OF 7 OUT OF 10 RACES INCLUDING: Dewhurst Stakes, Derby Stakes, Irish Derby, King George VI and Queen Elizabeth Stakes.

NIJINSKY
Bay Colt 1967

Northern Dancer	Nearctic	Nearco	
(b.1961)		Lady Angela	
	Natalma	Native Dancer	
		Almahmoud	
Flaming Page	Bull Page	Bull Lea	
(b.1959)		Our Page	
	Flaring Top	Menow	
		Flaming Top	

BRED: EDWARD TAYLOR (CAN.). WINNER OF 11 OUT OF 13 RACES INCLUDING: Dewhurst Stakes, 2000 Guineas Stakes, Derby Stakes, Irish Derby, King George VI and Queen Elizabeth Stakes, St. Leger Stakes.

RIVERMAN
Bay Colt 1969

Never Bend	Nasrullah	Nearco	
(b.1960)		Mumtaz Begum	
	Lalun	Djeddah	
		Be Faithful	
River Lady	Prince John	Princequillo	
(b.1963)		Not Afraid	
	Nile Lily	Roman	
		Azalea	

BRED: HARRY GUGGENHEIM (USA). WINNER OF 5 OUT OF 8 STARTS INCLUDING: Poule d'Essai des Poulains, Prix d'Ispahan, Prix Jean Prat.

SEA BIRD II
Chestnut Colt 1962

Dan Cupid	Native Dancer	Polynesian	
(ch.1956)		Geisha	
	Vixenette	Sickle	
		Lady Reynard	
Sicalade	Sicambre	Prince Bio	
(b.1956)		Sif	
	Marmelade	Maurepas	
		Couleur	

BRED: JEAN TERYNCK (FR.). WINNER OF 7 OUT OF 8 RACES INCLUDING: Derby Stakes, Prix Lupin, Grand Prix de Saint-Cloud, Prix de L'Arc de Triomphe.

SECRETARIAT
Chestnut Colt 1970

Bold Ruler	Nasrullah	Nearco	
(b.1954)		Mumtaz Begum	
	Miss Disco	Discovery	
		Outdone	
Something Royal	Princequillo	Prince Rose	
(b.1952)		Cosquilla	
	Imperatrice	Caruso	
		Cinquepace	

BRED: MEADOW STUD (USA). WINNER OF 16 OUT OF 21 RACES INCLUDING: Kentucky Derby Stakes, Belmont Stakes, Preakness Stakes, Arlington Invitational Stakes, Marlboro Cup Invitational Stakes, Man O'War Stakes.

SHIRLEY HEIGHTS
Bay Colt 1975

Mill Reef	Never Bend	Nasrullah	
(b.1968)		Lalun	
	Milan Mill	Princequillo	
		Virginia Water	
Hardiemma	Hardicanute	Hard Ridden	
(b.1969)		Harvest Maid	
	Grand Cross	Grandmaster	
		Blue Cross	

BRED: LORD HALIFAX and LORD IRWIN (UK). WINNER OF 6 OUT OF 11 RACES INCLUDING: Royal Lodge Stakes, Dante Stakes, Derby Stakes, Irish Derby.

TRANSCRIPT'S BREEDING

THE HORSE we chose to follow from Clive Brittain's table was Transcript, a nice two-year old filly owned by Geoffrey Hughes and assigned to the care of stable lad Rick Owen. It had not been our intention to fasten our sights upon a superhorse. Clive, as it turned out, had a particularly fine batch of two-year olds that year (one of them, Mystiko, was to win the 2,000 Guineas as a three-year old the following season) and no doubt we could have latched on to one of them. But Transcript seemed perfect for what we wanted – an average sort of racehorse with average prospects – and we looked forward to following her career with the same sort of enthusiasm as is experienced by the average owner.

Things at first were not to turn out as we either hoped or expected. All sorts of variants, and in particular the weather, combined to conspire against us. At first we cursed our luck and felt a mounting frustration. Then we began to realise that in Transcript's career we had found exactly what we had been looking for – an average career with all the attendant worries, disappointments and anxieties, and, just occasionally, that wonderful burst of elation.

Note: Transcript's sire, Transworld, was an Irish-trained colt who, in 1977, was rated at 123 in the International Classifications (the highest rating so far has been the 141 awarded to Dancing Brave in 1986).

THIS PEDIGREE IS AN EXTRACT FROM STUD BOOK RECORDS AND IS NOT A CERTIFICATE OF IDENTITY

Sire:- TRANSWORLD (USA)

(CH 1974)

PRINCE JOHN

HORNPIPE

TRANSCRIPT (GB)   BAY FILLY

Foaled in 1988

Dam:- LAWYER'S WAVE (USA)

(B 1975)

ADVOCATOR

FLEETSIDE

WEATHERBYS

Information Services Department

Sanders Road, Wellingborough
Northamptonshire NN8 4BX
Telephone Wellingborough (0933) 440077

NCEQUILLO
- Prince Rose
  - Rose Prince
  - Indolence
- Cosquilla
  - Papyrus
  - Quick Thought

T AFRAID
- Count Fleet
  - Reigh Count
  - Quickly
- Banish Fear
  - Blue Larkspur
  - Herodiade

HORNBEAM
- Hyperion
  - Gainsborough
  - Selene
- Thicket
  - Nasrullah
  - Thorn Wood

SUGAR BUN
- Mahmoud
  - Blenheim
  - Mah Mahal
- Galatea II
  - Dark Legend
  - Galaday II

ROUND TABLE
- Princequillo
  - Prince Rose
  - Cosquilla
- Knight's Daughter
  - Sir Cosmo
  - Feola

DELTA QUEEN
- Bull Lea
  - Bull Dog
  - Rose Leaves
- Bleebok
  - Blue Larkspur
  - Forteresse

FLEET NASRULLAH
- Nasrullah
  - Nearco
  - Mumtaz Begum
- Happy Go Fleet
  - Count Fleet
  - Draeh

FARSIDE
- Khaled
  - Hyperion
  - Eclair
- Dark Diana
  - Count Gallahad
  - Reigh Diana

The firm of Weatherbys has been the Jockey Club's secretariat since 1770, but has recently shed its old-fashioned image in favour of one more in keeping with the age of high technology. They deal with much of racing's day-to-day administration as well as acting as keeper of the records and producer of various publications, including the General Stud Book and the Racing Calendar.

PLANTATION STUD

LORD HOWARD de Walden's immaculate Plantation Stud, just outside Newmarket, is the home of his 1985 Derby winner and stallion Slip Anchor. Lord Howard bought his dam Sayonara from the famous German Schlenderhan Stud and put her to the 1978 Derby winner and top stallion, Shirley Heights, himself a son of the great Mill Reef and an inmate of the Royal Stud at Sandringham.

Lord Howard de Walden stands five stallions in which he is the major shareholder: Kris, Shavian, Slip Anchor, Diesis and Pharly, as well as having shares in fourteen other stallions. He owns 26 broodmares, three studs and, in 1991, had 43 horses in training: 19 with Henry Cecil, 11 with Willie Jarvis, and 6 with Julie Cecil, all at Newmarket; 2 with Peter Walwyn in Lambourn; 3 fillies with Brian Mayfield-Smith in Australia; and 2 jumpers with trainer Charlie Brooks in Lambourn.

LORD HOWARD DE WALDEN

One of the most successful owner/breeders and one of the best-known personalities on the turf is Lord Howard de Walden. Lord Howard is one of the few breeders in the country still to rear all his own horses and seldom put them through the sales as yearlings. He has this in common with the Queen but, unlike Her Majesty, realized his dream of many years in 1985 when he won the Derby with his home-bred colt, Slip Anchor, after 40 years of trying.

The continuing importance of the Epsom Derby, despite its slide down the scale of the world's richest races to about thirtieth place, and despite the growing international challenge to its status, puts one in mind of the comment made by Frederico Tesio, the great breeder of Ribot, which sums up so well the difficult and chancy game: "The

Thoroughbred exists because its selection has depended not on experts, technicians or zoologists but on a piece of wood: the winning post of the Derby."

Twice Senior Steward of the Jockey Club, Lord Howard has an enormous enthusiasm for racing which he has maintained in full over a long life. The foundation of his great success as a breeder was laid when he bought a group of first-rate mares from Lady Sassoon in the 1960s, including Soft Angels, the champion two-year-old filly of 1965. Soft Angels's second foal was Doubly Sure who, despite failing to win a race, was wisely allowed to prove herself as a broodmare. She returned the favour a thousandfold by producing Kris, the European champion miler of 1979 and Diesis, the European champion two-year-old of 1982.

◀
Slip Anchor at Plantation Stud. Winner of the Derby, his value on syndication was put at £5.4 million.

◀◀
Slip Anchor at Plantation Stud.

▼
Mill Reef, one of the greatest horses of the post-war era, was generously allowed to stand at stud in Britain by his anglophile American owner, Paul Mellon. His statue now graces his last home, the National Stud at Newmarket.

Slip Anchor will cover some 50 mares each season at a fee of £20,000 a time if the mare is in foal on October 1st. His valuation at the time of his syndication, when 31 of 40 shares were sold, was £5.4 million. He covers a mare at 10 in the morning, and/or at 3 in the afternoon. Occasionally he will cover a third at 8 in the evening. Mares and foals usually go out all day, weather permitting, until 3.30 in the afternoon. Some mares are boxed out to other stallions in the area, covered and boxed back again. Next door to the good-sized stable where a mare about to foal is waiting for the onset of birth pangs there is nearly always a member of staff spending all night in the "sitting-up" room, a comfortable enough billet with kettle, fire, stove, TV and radio.

Some of the foals are weaned at Plantation Stud, especially some of the earlier ones, but the bulk are sent north to Thornton Stud for that purpose, where they remain until the middle of November when they are sent down to Lord Howard's private stud at Hungerford, Berkshire, to be joined by the foals from five mares based in America. There they stay until the following August when, now yearlings, they return to Plantation. They are not broken at Plantation except in the case of a large stroppy colt, for example, who would be a danger to himself and everything else in the paddock, when a start might be made.

The covering season lasts officially from February 15th to July 15th. Effectively it may start a few days earlier and ends in the first week in June. No foal may be born before January 1st, the date in the northern hemisphere when all Thoroughbreds have their birthdays. The day starts at 7.30 when the staff start trying the mares with the teaser, a luckless animal whose lot it is to establish whether a mare will be receptive to the attentions of the stallion, risks a severe kicking if she is not and who himself never reaps his just reward. When it has been established whether the mare is coming into season or whether she has broken, a visit by the vet follows, and mares are covered generally on his advice. Mares on the premises would include some of Lord Howard's and others sent by owners for Slip Anchor's services. In May 1991, for example, two of Lord Howard's mares were visiting Kris at Thornton Stud, Yorkshire, along with two late-foaling mares. There were two mares who foaled at home and then went to Ireland with foals at foot, and the rest were at Plantation Stud visiting Slip Anchor or other stallions.

RUNNING A STUD

PLANTATION Stud is managed by Leslie Harrison, who has been in the job since 1973 and also acts as Lord Howard de Walden's racing manager. Under him there is a staff of eight, led by the stud groom Pat Burstow. There are 150 acres, which at the busiest time of year are home to between 60 and 70 mares and foals. As in the better racing stables, the staff at a good stud like Plantation are remarkable for their hard work and dedication, driven not by the size of their pay-packets but by their genuine love for horses. Pat Burstow is at work at 6.30 on most days and is present at every foaling, most of which take place in the middle of the night. The staff take turns in "sitting-up" nearly every night between January

▲
Lleyty Stud, in south Wales.

▲
Mtoto, Michael Roberts up, wins the Prince of Wales Stakes at Ascot.

▼
Slip Anchor at Plantation Stud.

and June. Some foalings are a great deal easier than others, but it is a rare thing at Plantation for the vet to be called in. The foals will then stay on their mother's milk for as long as they are left to do so, and will normally start to be weaned at about five months.

Pat's life is made slightly easier by the fact that Slip Anchor is a stallion with a sweet-natured temperament whose ability to cover mares, and fertility, are very good. Steve Murray, who has been part of the team at Plantation since leaving school in 1980, corroborates this: "He must be one of the best horses for covering in Newmarket." Like so many people in racing, Steve works hard for what some might consider meazly pay, but he is quick to point to the satisfaction his job brings him, both in working with horses, and in watching the whole cycle of a horse's career, from the day it is foaled, through its racecourse career to its days as a stallion or brood mare, when the chances are it may even return once more to Plantation Stud. "That's a great thing," he comments. "That's what keeps you going. After all, mucking out every day's not such a wonderful job." Four lads live on the stud with their families in houses provided by Lord Howard, and four lads live off the premises.

Even when the busy time of year is over in theory, there are always any number of maintenance jobs to be getting on with around the premises. And then almost as soon as the foals have gone away the yearlings are arriving. Slip Anchor himself is on an easy routine between July and November and is usu-

▲
The stallion Slew O' Gold in Kentucky.

◀
Mtoto arriving at his owner's stud, wearing protective bandages from the journey.

ally turned out during the day. He pines a bit during the off-season, missing the mares, and doesn't do himself quite so well. Then before Christmas he starts to be prepared for the season. A stallion has to be fit to do his job and is lunged and hand-led out at exercise for about two hours a day.

Like most stud staff, Pat Burstow gets tremendous satisfaction out of watching the careers of the animals he has been so closely involved with. He does not believe it is possible to tell a winner at birth, but that it's easy enough to spot a loser. Then again he recalls that Doubly Sure's first foal, the Champion Miler Kris, had very bad hindlegs and could not even stand during his first 24 hours. As a foal you would have given him no chance, and he was still not liked by anybody as a yearling. It was only when he went into training that he started looking like a racehorse. Pat sums up the art of training concisely: "A good trainer can win with a bad horse, and a bad trainer can ruin a good one."

BREEDING A WINNER

LORD HOWARD bought Plantation in 1958 from Lord Derby and ran it initially as a private stud. Lord Howard and Leslie Harrison wanted to stand a stallion at Plantation and always lived in the belief that they would breed a horse good enough, but this looked less and less likely as the years went by. In 1978 they bought Dance in Time, the champion Canadian three-year-old and the last relatively cheap son of the soon-to-be-fabled Northern Dancer. He was syndicated at £8,000 a share and remained at Plantation for six years. He had his moments, but was never a startling success, though he never failed to fill his book, and he was sold on for £20,000 a share to go to California.

Plantation went for a year without a stallion and then bought Pharly, who had been French Champion Sire a couple of times and was resyndicated in England. He stood at Plantation for two seasons and then moved to Beech House, and

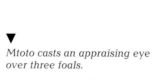

A peaceful summer scene of mares and foals in the paddocks at Hesmond Stud.

▼ *Mtoto casts an appraising eye over three foals.*

then Woodlands, to make way for Slip Anchor. A Derby winner, especially one as beautifully-bred as Slip Anchor, starts his stud career with a considerable advantage, but just like every other stallion he has to prove himself in the ever-increasingly competitive world of breeding. But it certainly helps to attract the best mares – the best producers rather than the best race mares. Slip Anchor

was in his fifth year at stud in 1991, "And from here on," in the words of Leslie Harrison, "it's up to him. He has always had a very high fertility and therefore enough foals on the ground, so now he'll either make it or he won't. This is his critical period."

Leslie Harrison has no recipe for success in the breeding game, none anyway that he can put into words. "You could, I suppose, work it out mechanically on blood affiliations," he muses, "but at the end of the day you're dealing with individuals, with temperament, make and shape, stamina and speed, and you have to try to keep an all-round view."

Even a breeder like Lord Howard de Walden cannot sit back and depend entirely on his home-bred stock. It is essential to keep changing the blood. The magic age with a mare is 11 or 12. A mare might be 9 by the time her second foal is a three-year-old, and the breeder might be getting an inkling by then of how good she is going to be as a brood mare. A certain number of moderate mares always slip through the culling net and in hindsight it is sometimes difficult to tell why, but culling, though crucial, is a difficult task (as the Queen's sale of Height of Fashion, subsequently dam of

because she was the only daughter Lord Howard had from Soft Angels. She was sent to the then locally-based and modestly priced (at £800 a nomination) stallion Sharpen Up. The result was Kris. "It wasn't a matter of pure luck, as nowadays is always said," says Harrison. "I like to think there was a certain amount of thought given to it, but it was certainly fortunate."

In the commercial modern world, when accusations of factory farming are levelled at the most productive of the huge Kentucky studs, Plantation Stud is a rarity, even an anachronism. Yet it is an operation which certainly produces results, and in Slip Anchor perhaps the greatest result of all.

Unfuwain and Nashwan, demonstrates) and there is many a stud that ought to practise it more.

The uncertainties of breeding are such that the best mare Lord Howard de Walden has ever had, Doubly Sure, had a Timeform rating of 51, suggesting that she would have had difficulty winning a selling race. Though she had plenty of ability at home, the moment she came off the bridle on a racecourse she found nothing. In the end she made heavy weather of coming second in the humble Beldale Plate at Thirsk – "in the middle of the night", as Lord Howard put it – for which distinction she gained the reward of £76. The only reason she was kept was

▶ *Second Lot leaves Clive Brittain's yard for the nearby gallops at Newmarket.*

SLIP ANCHOR'S PEDIGREE				Never Bend

Slip Anchor is bred in the purple. Both his sire, Shirley Heights, and his grandsire, Mill Reef, won the Derby, and have gone on to prove themselves as two of the most successful stallions standing in England in the last two decades, though sadly Mill Reef is no more. Slip Anchor was in his fifth year at stud in 1991, and, in the matter-of-fact words of his Stud Manager, "From here on it's up to him."

SLIP ANCHOR	Shirley Heights	Mill Reef	Never Bend
Bay Colt 1982	(b.1975)	Hardiemma	Milan Mill
	Sayonara	Birkhahn	Hardicanute
	(b.1965)	Suleika	Grand Cross
			Alchimist
			Bramouse
			Ticino
			Schwarzblaurot

BRED: LORD HOWARD DE WALDEN (UK). WINNER OF 4 OUT OF 9 RACES INCLUDING: Lingfield Derby Trial Stakes, Derby Stakes.

THE STABLES

CLIVE BRITTAIN'S YARD

CLIVE BRITTAIN is one of the most successful trainers in the British Isles. From his beautifully-appointed Carlburg Stables on Newmarket's Bury Road he regularly saddles about 40 winners a year for a long list of patrons that includes the Dowager Lady Beaverbrook and Sheikh Mohammed, the world's leading owner.

It was for the Sheikh that Clive trained the great filly Pebbles who is still the

▼ *Some of Clive Brittain's string at exercise at Newmarket.*

Former stable lad Clive Brittain has built up one of the most successful yards in Britain. He has the reputation of never being afraid to try his horses in the best company and has sometimes been scorned for doing so. His remarkable list of victories, however, including three Classics with Julio Mariner, Pebbles and Mystiko, shows the wisdom of his ways. Brittain has also achieved the remarkable – and possibly unique – feat of being universally liked by all sections of the horse racing profession.

leading British-trained money earner of all time. She won the 1,000 Guineas (Clive's second Classic win), the Eclipse Stakes and the Champion Stakes before defying all received wisdom and crossing to the United States to pull off a thrilling victory in the Breeders Cup Turf. Clive is the one and only British trainer to achieve this outstanding feat, as he is also to be the winner of another of the world's richest races, the Japan Cup, a prize he lifted in 1986 with the seven-year-old former handicapper, Jupiter Island.

As these stunning successes prove, Clive is not one to sit on his laurels, but is constantly searching for new targets, and he is never afraid to try his horses among the best company, a policy at which some have levelled criticism but which, as the statistics show, reaps its just reward. He is that rarity among fashionable Newmarket trainers, someone who has

▶ *Newmarket. Traffic traditionally gives way to horses as they cross the road. Indeed, at Newmarket everything and everybody gives way to horses.*

worked his way up from the bottom to the very top. Born in Calne in Wiltshire, he served his apprenticeship with Sir Noel Murless, the greatest of British post-war trainers, and rose to become the head lad at Warren Place before starting off on his own. This spectacular career explains not only why Clive knows every facet of the racing game, but also why his staff are generally considered to be the happiest, best looked after and, perhaps as a consequence of this, the hardest working in Newmarket.

"The structure of the stable is like this, "says Brittain. "I have an assistant, Jock Brown, a travelling head lad, John Spouse, a second travelling head lad, Sue Davidson, then Jimmy Miller, Mick Leaman and Harold Moss who are all head men. So there is a senior staff of about ten who take care of the feeding and do most of the running around and chasing everybody.

"A good feeder is very important. Mick Leaman certainly knows his horses, and part of the secret of success is not overfacing a horse that's not doing too well. I have an in-house farrier too, Nick Furlong. He services 165 horses and that keeps his back bent."

1990 was an average sort of year for Brittain's Carlburg Stable, and it broke down as follows. His 41 two-year olds ran 140 races for 13 victories, 31 places and a level stakes loss of £62.24. For his 45 three-year olds the figures were 216, 18, 41 and a loss of £12.95, for his 26 older horses the figures were 147, 10, 23, and a loss of £25.67.

The best months for his two-year olds were June, July and August, and he gained 3 wins from 23 races with them in each. For his three-year olds, August was the best month, producing 5 wins from 29 attempts, and his older horses flourished particularly in the same month, gaining 3 victories from 19 starts. None of his two-year olds won over a longer distance than a mile, and none of his three-year olds at less than 7 furlongs. His older horses, however, won at most distances raced.

Twenty-four of the stable's victories came in conditions races and 17 of them in handicaps. The strike level was in general better for the latter, however, and the three-year old handicappers, with 9 wins from 79 starts, returned a level stakes profit of £38.

By far the largest number of winners, 23, came at Group One racecourses, where the vast majority of the horses were run, with 6 at Group Two, 9 at Group Three and only 3 at Group Four. The highest number of wins – 8 – came at the local course, Newmarket, where the stable had by far the most runners. The next most-used track was Ascot, which yielded 3 wins. The best strike rate of 50 per cent was attained at the smaller courses of Beverley, Brighton and Hamilton. Clive had winners at 14 other courses, including 4 at unique Chester, and failed to score at 16 others, including both all-weather courses.

In all, 34 separate horses won for the yard, 7 of them twice and the rest once only, for 24 owners. Seven scored at the first time of asking. Clive's horses started as favourites only 20 times, winning on 6 occasions. The average starting price was 9.4/1. Total winning prize money was £332,771, for which the yard had once to endure a losing sequence of 55 races. Michael Roberts was by far the most employed jockey, winning 29 races from 226 rides. Seven other jockeys won for the stable and 36 others failed to do so.

◀ *Clive Brittain.*

▼ *Italian Newmarket-based trainer Luca Cumani, with hack and goat.*

THE TRAINER'S DAY

NO ONE at Carlburg stables works harder than Clive himself. He gets up most of the year long before dawn and his first lot is invariably the earliest each morning on the Newmarket gallops. At the height of the training programme he sends out four lots (*see p59*) a day. His stable now has about 140 boxes split between two yards, one housing the two-year-olds and one the older horses. Facilities include an indoor ride and an equine swimming pool. He also keeps another 40 horses in two satellite yards, making about 180 in all. He currently employs a staff of 73.

"My day starts at about quarter past four when I get up, and I'm in the yard by 4.30. I check the horses while the feeders go about their business, and then the staff arrive about 5.30 at the latest, though the majority are quite a lot earlier than that.

CLIVE BRITTAIN'S SUMMER ROUTINE

4.15	Gets up.
4.30	Gets to the yard to check the horses.
5.30	Pulls out with the first lot.
6.30	Fits in a few early phone calls.
7.00	Pulls out with the second lot.
9.00	Breakfast and more phone calls.
10.00	Pulls out with the third lot.
11.30	Possibly oversees the fourth lot or more likely gets in the car to visit other horses elsewhere. Off to the races on racing days.
15.30	Back in the yard to see the horses whenever possible.
16.30	Off by car to see the other horses.
17.30	Back in the yard to finish off evening stables.
18.15	More phone calls.
20.00	Dinner.

"The first lot pulls out at 5.40, or 5.30 in the summer. Then we work the first and second lots before stopping for breakfast at 9. I might make a couple of phone calls after the first lot and the rest I make during breakfast, when of course people also know that they'll find me in. Then we go out with the third lot before 10 o'clock and there's usually a fourth. I make use of most of the gallops at Newmarket. I go to the Racecourse Side in the spring but in particular I favour the Limekilns. We usually work the horses in lots of about 50. I ride out with three lots here, then I get in the car and go and see the other horses in the satellites.

"In the winter I might not get up until about 5.30, and wouldn't be in the yard until 5.45. Then the first lot wouldn't pull out until 6.15, still pretty early, and there'd be two more lots after that.

"In the afternoon I'm in the yard at 3.30 to see the horses, then again I get in

the car and go and see the others. I'm back in the yard for the rest of evening stables, finishing about 6. Then there are phone calls for about half an hour, a glass of wine and dinner.

"With the Satellite Information Services installation I've cut back on the number of times I go racing per week to about four. When I go racing at a course that is any distance away I often fly from the July Course (at Newmarket), but I still invariably have to miss seeing the last lot.

"I also have to go to all the main sales, including the Keeneland summer sale in America. I don't usually go to the Keeneland September sale, however, because there are ample autumn sales in England to buy and sell enough horses.

"The stable has about 40 different owners at present. Nearly all of them have been with me for many years, though I have a few new ones as well".

▼
André Fabre, one of the most successful French trainers, shepherded Arazi through his unbeaten two-year old career, ending up with his triumph in the Breeders Cup series in the USA.

RUNNING THE YARD

Most trainers of any worth will acknowledge the fact that the secret of a successful stable is team effort, and the more dedicated and skilful the staff, the more successful the yard. At the top of the pyramid is the trainer himself. He must take ultimate responsibility for all that happens on or off the premises, and it is he who receives the accolades of victory and the brickbats of failure.

Under him there will be an assistant trainer, whose job it is to run the yard in the trainer's absence and to represent him elsewhere, including at the races, when necessary. There may also be a pupil assistant. Then there is the head lad, in many ways the most important person in the yard after the trainer himself. It is he who oversees much of the day to day running of the yard and who knows most about what is going on, who is pulling their weight and who is not. Like all successful operations, a successful yard is a happy one. A large yard may well have more than one lad with the prefix "head", denoting seniority and extra responsibilities.

▶
Feeding time at the yard.

▶ ▶
Charlie Whittingham with Sunday Silence.

▼
Keeping the horses well groomed is a vital part of the yard's day-to-day activities.

Then there are the lads themselves, each "doing" their three horses and riding and mucking out and lending a hand with various other jobs round the yard. One, two or more of them, depending on the size of the stable, will be designated "travelling head lad", and will spend much of their lives during the racing season travelling to and from the races with the horses.

Most yards have one or more secretaries to cope with the paperwork, the entries, the phone calls and the fax machine, among many other duties. Some stables will also employ or part-employ a formbook expert to help with the placing of the horses in races. The larger yards will have a vet and blacksmith on more or less permanent duty.

No lover of horse racing should miss the chance of visiting a stable, and those of us who do not do so in the normal run of events would be well-advised to take advantage of the many "open days" staged by some of the biggest names in training. Usually in the cause of charity, the likes of Henry Cecil and John Dunlop open their yards to the paying public and make sure that many of the star inmates are on hand.

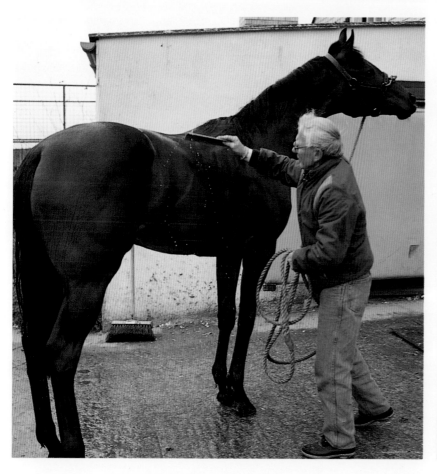

THE SECRETARY

Karen Saunders is one of two secretaries attached to Clive Brittain's Carlburg yard.

"During the racing season I work from 8.30 until 5. First of all I go through the declarations with Mr Brittain, then I ring up Weatherbys and declare the horses and whether they're wearing blinkers and so on. I do this as early as possible, and always by 10 o'clock, so that nothing gets forgotten. I arrange jockeys where necessary, usually with the jockey's agent. Then I ring up the owners and let them know where and when their horses are running and who's riding. Then we do the entries that need to be made that morning, as well as taking a number of calls that are always coming in. And again, the owners have to be informed about their horses' plans.

"That takes care of an often quite hectic morning, and although I don't have that much contact with the horses themselves, my office looks out over the yard, so I can see them and what's going on.

"The afternoons are usually nice and quiet. It's mostly a question of keeping things up to date, like vaccinations, veterinary records, the comings and goings of the staff and all the paperwork that goes with it all.

"During the winter, in the close season, things obviously wind down a bit. There is the occasional runner on the all-weather tracks, certain foreign entries to be made, and of course all the new intakes of horses have to be catalogued. We keep a record of when they arrive, their pedigrees, their passports and vaccinations.

"I am one of two secretaries employed by the stable, and nowadays modern technology has made things very different from a few years ago. Now we have two computers, a fax machine, a telex and a photocopier. But the telephone is still the most important and useful instrument of all.

"I came straight from school into this job and wouldn't have another. I love it and get quite involved with all the horses and people in the yard."

THE ASSISTANT TRAINER

JOCK BROWN is Clive Brittain's assistant. In many of the large and fashionable yards, the post of assistant trainer is seen as a temporary stop on the road to setting up as trainer in your own right. Recent examples have been Willie Jarvis (formerly assistant to Henry Cecil) and James Fanshawe (Michael Stoute). The talented assistant trainer will not only learn his craft from an acknowledged master, but will also make any number of useful contacts in the racing world (including owners who may send him horses when he starts up on his own). They are often seen at the races supervizing the horses when their masters are elsewhere. Clive Brittain tends to rely on travelling head lads to go to the races in his stead, and therefore Jock Brown's role as assistant is different. He is effectively Clive's right-hand man in running the yard, and Brown seldom goes to the races himself.

"My day starts in the yard at about 4.30 with the head lads, when we give the horses their early feed. When they're all fed we get the tack together and pull out about 5.45 for the first lot. We're out for about an hour and a half, till 7.15. Then we take the second lot out just after half-past, come back for breakfast, take the third lot out just after 9.30 and get in about 11. Then we check round to make sure all the horses are all right, and Mick Leaman stops here and feeds them while the rest of us are away.

"We've recently made the change to newspaper for the horses' bedding. Last year we found that we got one good load

JAMES FANSHAWE

One of the fastest rising stars among the list of younger trainers is the painstaking and gifted Newmarket handler James Fanshawe. Formerly assistant to Michael Stoute, his exploits with Environment Friend in 1991 gained him many new admirers.

In his first season of 1990 he clocked up 18 winners from 113 races to show a level stakes profit of £58.96, one of the few figures he is unlikely to improve on in the future, as punters will soon be aware of his shrewdness and ability.

of straw and two bad loads. The bad loads were very dusty. Many problems are caused to horses by dust. Horses are really just lungs on legs, and dust easily gets up their noses and into those lungs. This paper is dust-free, so we thought we'd give it a try, though it's a bit more expensive. It's clean, it's dry, and it's warm, and you know what you're getting each time. Some of the other stables use paper too, like Luca Cumani's and Michael Stoute's.

"I and the head men return about 3pm and we check round the horses. We make sure all of them have eaten up and look for any problems for Mr Brittain to

▼ *Chimes of Freedom* (far side), *Mutah* (centre) *and North Country* (near side) *on the exercise gallop on Newmarket Heath.*

investigate when he comes round for evening stables. I'm usually finished by 6. There's more to do in the spring than in the summer, doing the groundwork. In fact spring is probably the busiest time of the year. After all, if a horse has just had a race, he'll probably just go out walking for half an hour and then go and pick grass in the paddock. That'll happen for two or three days.

"I always go to Newmarket, otherwise I don't go racing very often. My responsibilities are almost entirely in the yard. This is a happy set-up and the lads get good bonuses and perks, which gives them a bit of incentive to work."

THE FEEDER

MICK LEAMAN is one of Clive Brittain's head men and is renowned as one of the best feeders in the business. Chief feeder is an especially important role in a stable, for obvious reasons.

"I feed all the horses myself. You get to know your animals and which one can eat what. If you've got a horse that's not eating very well, then you have to change its feed around a bit, make it a bit sweeter. The main factor is to keep a horse eating, especially in the spring, when we are trying to build them up.

"When they start doing some hard gallops they may go off their food, so we get as much as we can into them early in the year. An average, decent-sized horse will eat about 18lbs of food a day, but a little filly wouldn't eat so much. A bad "doer" might be down to 12lbs. That's all right if she's not being made to do too much. The guv'nor would train her accordingly and leave her alone to bring her back on her food.

"So an average horse would eat around 18lbs of corn a day and at night would get some bran mixed in with it. And for the midday feed I mix it down with garlic honey and salt. Sometimes I might even use Epsom salts just to cool the blood down. At night time they all get much the same quantity, and at midday I catch up with some of my best doers. That feed takes me about two hours to get round. At midday everything is mixed together, but at night they get perhaps three bowls of dry corn, and a handful of perhaps 2lbs of bran made down with molasses. And we've started using blood salts now after a few problems with the horses' blood. It smells like aniseed, a bit sharpish, and they won't eat it by itself. In fact it's just dried blood.

"In the winter the two-year-olds also get extra vitamins via calcium and bonemeal to build them up and harden their bones. And we use a lot of cod liver oil, which is a particularly good combination with molasses. And when they start racing we come on to some stronger stuff, things like Hemopar, a liquid form of vitamin, and Twydil, a pellet form. Both give energy, and we take them off the growth promoters then. And the guv'nor gives me a list of about 30 horses he wants to be put on draught Guinness. I

► *Mick Leaman, renowned chief feeder at Clive Brittain's Carlburg Stables.*

don't know if it does any good. I think sometimes if you've got a bad doer it brings them on to their feed. They seem to enjoy it.

"In the morning they start off with one bowl of corn. We just give them that as we go round to check they've eaten up overnight. They get that at about 4.30 when about five of us come round and check them. It's after that that I mix the main midday feed. And I ride out one lot. It used to be two, but they've cut me down as I just couldn't do it. I even feed the horses stabled in the two studs as well. I use up almost 2 tons of corn a day.

▼ *The most important time of day.*

▲
Competing for the Ormonde Stakes at Chester.

"When a horse comes back from a race it's only on a small feed, and we give it a couple of days to pick up again. Of course, some are really tough animals and won't leave anything. But most of them will leave a bit, especially if they've had a hard race. You don't really want them to leave anything, because you've got to try and keep their condition. To some extent the guv'nor can train them to the feedhouse. If a horse isn't "doing" all right then he'll probably decide to leave it alone.

"Though I'm a head lad, I'm left alone to do the feeding. I was in catering in the army so I should know a bit about it. And I always like to have a horse to look after too. I've been quite successful with them in the past, having looked after Supreme Leader, Julio Mariner, the St. Leger winner, and Mark Anthony, who beat Grundy in the Greenham Stakes at Newbury. You get a lot out of having a good horse, and the main problem is keeping them sound. So many good ones go wrong.

"All in all I'd agree that I have a hard day's work, if you like. But I don't go out, I don't drink and I don't smoke. I just keep going."

▶ *Returning from the gallops at Clive Brittain's yard.*

◀ *Rick Owen with Transcript.*

THE STABLE LAD

RICK OWEN is the stable lad who "does" Transcript and two other horses. The stable lad (the name "lad" is applied to both male and female staff, irrespective of age) is on the bottom rung of the ladder. He is badly paid and expected to work extremely hard. He not only looks after his three horses, more in some yards, but also rides out two, three or even four lots on work days, and goes to the races when his charge is running. Neither are his weekends periods of uninterrupted free time, as horses don't look after themselves. At their best, stable lads are remarkable people, giving a life's hard service for little return, quite often for the simple reason that they love being with horses.

"I've been in various yards before Mr Brittain's, and this would be a good job as far as jobs in racing go. He's got good staff, and the main reason for this is that he treats them well and is pleasant to them. On the other hand we work harder at the Carlburg stables than most of the other stables in town.

"Clive changes the times, but in general we're at work at 5 o'clock during the racing season. We ride work on Tuesdays, Wednesdays, Fridays and Saturdays normally, because it's such a large yard. The first lot do proper work, and the second and third are just trotters and canterers.

"I look after three horses at the moment. Two are very nice fillies and I'm particularly fond of Transcript, who I'm sure will pick up a little race eventually. (This interview took place in February 1991.) She's a real character. She's a brave old girl and I think the world of her. Some lads get attached to their horses and some don't. I'm fairly laid back and don't normally get involved with them. Some you're glad to see the back of to tell the truth. But with some, like Transcript, you form an understanding, a partnership. They do everything bar talk to you.

"Between the second and third lots we have breakfast in the canteen. There are probably about 40 of us at a time there. Very often there's a fourth lot to ride out. Clive gets the work out of you, there's no doubt about that. He's a very clever man, actually. He pays a good wage, but you probably do more work than it warrants. But he's a very pleasant man and a good one to work for, and the lads don't mind. And we still finish early, though we're in early too.

"At the moment we're just starting to pick the horses up a little and do a bit more with them. In the mornings we're finishing between 11 and 11.30. Then you go home and do what you want. Some rush home and some stroll.

"I take a great pleasure in the horses but I'm not keen on going racing, unlike most of the lads, because I don't like travelling. I've just bought myself a house and I've got a lot of work to do there in the afternoons, so that keeps me busy. When I do go racing I'm not particularly good with time, and I'm always late or early coming into the paddock.

"In the afternoons the lads return for evening stables at about 3.30, me at about a minute to 4. Clive very rarely looks round, but he likes to know that the job is done properly. He trusts his lads, and he's lucky enough to be able to. He comes and has a look, but a lot of trainers like you to stand the horses for them, and you wait for hours for them to come round. Clive likes to get done and get finished. He's not bothered about a few shavings in the tail.

"I started off in racing when I was 16 and I'm 25 now. I'll stay in racing because I enjoy it. I love being with horses and, quite honestly, I'm lucky to get paid for it."

SECOND TRAVELLING HEAD LAD

Sue Davidson is Clive Brittain's second travelling head lad. This long-winded appellation means exactly what it says. She will spend much of the season travelling: whenever, in fact, the stable has horses entered for races at more than one course. John Spouse is first travelling head lad. He will accompany the horses to the more important of the two or more meetings, and Sue will often find herself travelling north in the horsebox, accompanied by the horses and a lad or two. This suits her well, as Haydock and Redcar are her favourite courses, and she prefers the northern tracks in general. "People are nicer up there," she asserts.

She clocks up a huge number of miles every year and will often be obliged to stay away from home for one or more nights. In the winter months, when there is very much less racing, her duties are similar to those of any other lad.

Sue is totally dedicated to horses and to horse racing and, like many at Carlburg Stables, has been with Clive Brittain for a long time. She first rode out for him as a 14-year-old schoolgirl and now, 14 years later, she has risen

to her present position of responsiblity. She cites Mountain Kingdom as the best horse she has "done" and claims she has no ambition to set up as a trainer in her own right. "That would be too much like hard work," she jokes, as though hard work were not the main ingredient in her busy career.

TRAVELLING HEAD LAD

The Travelling Head Lad must have various qualities. He or she must be able to shoulder responsibility, for it is he who must ensure that everything goes right for the horses not only on the racecourse but also on the way there and back. In this day and age it is not uncommon to be travelling in a horsebox along with several hundreds of thousands of pounds worth of often tense and nervous horse.

He or she must also be prepared to travel many thousands of miles each year, often in cramped conditions and at horsebox speed, and also be prepared to stay away from home for one or more nights at a time on numerous occasions. And nobody would pretend that the average racecourse hostel is any better than adequate in its facilities, while some are decidedly worse than that.

He or she must also be ready to deal with any number of emergencies that may spring up at haphazard moments during a long season. The stable jockey is injured in the second race and a stand-in must be found, booked and declared at short notice. A horse might bolt going down to the start and do an unscheduled lap of the course. Has it taken too much out of itself before the race? It may be up to the Travelling Head Lad, as the trainer's on course representative, to make the vital decision of whether to scratch it from the race or let it take its chance. There may be large amounts of money and lesser or greater reputations at stake.

In gambling stables the Travelling Head Lad will often have been entrusted with wagers from the other lads. He or she not only has to try and 'get on' at the best price, or more likely organise someone else to do so, but also make the occasional impossibly difficult decision of deciding not to risk the money after all, suspecting that the horse is not completely right, only to watch it canter up unchallenged to the winning post a few minutes later. Then the long journey back to the stable and the disappointment of one's colleagues can seem especially irksome.

▶
Sue Davidson, Clive Brittain's second Travelling Head Lad, sees to one of the horses in the stable.

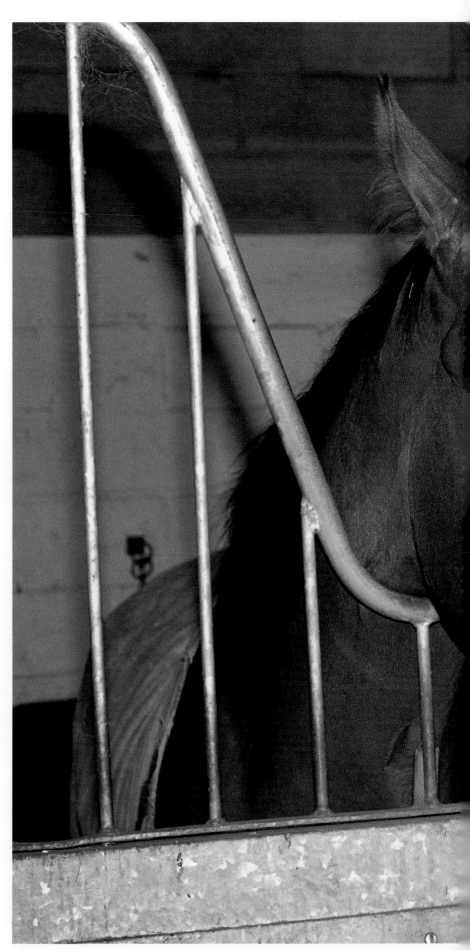

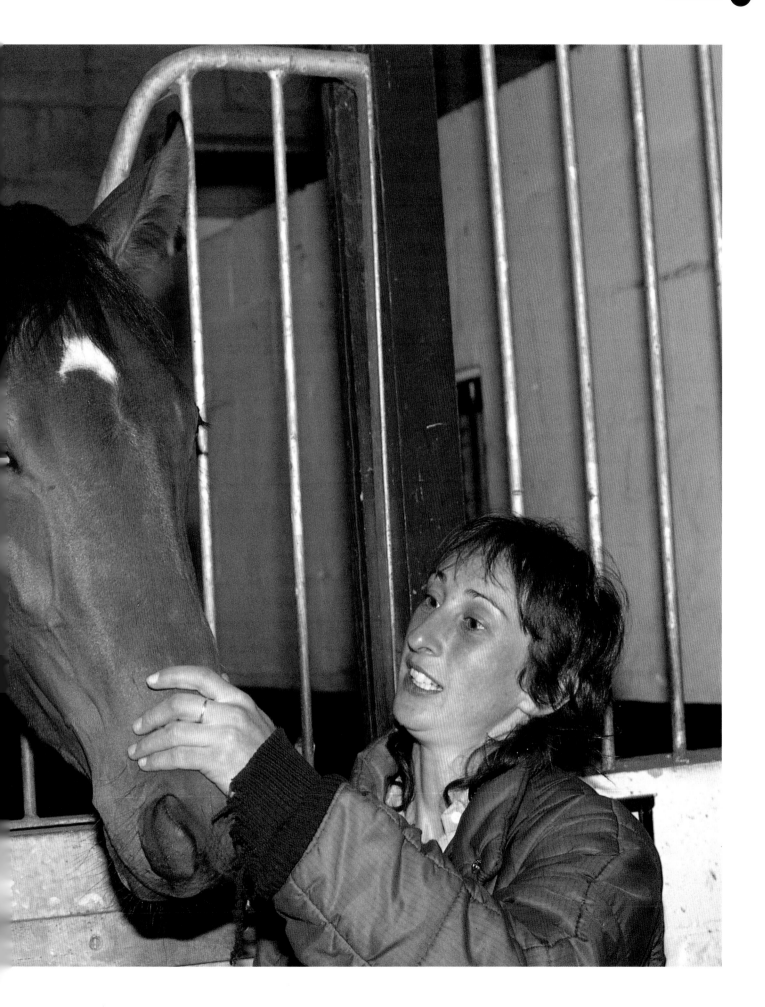

THE FARRIER'S CRAFT

Some of the biggest yards retain their own farrier. Other yards get freelance farriers in on a regular basis or when necessary. So the profession of farriery is thriving in and around the big training centres such as Lambourn, Newmarket, Malton and Middleham.

There is always at least one farrier present at every race-meeting too, there to deal with the eventuality of spread plates or other problems before a race, and to be available at the start to do any jobs that are required. Nick Furlong is nearly always in attendance at Newmarket racecourse and points out that there is a difference between dealing with horses that are calm enough in the environment of their own stable, but who can be tensed-up and nervous before the start of a race and who, with one kick, can cause serious injury.

Nick Furlong, farrier, goes about his morning's work at Clive Brittain's Newmarket stables.

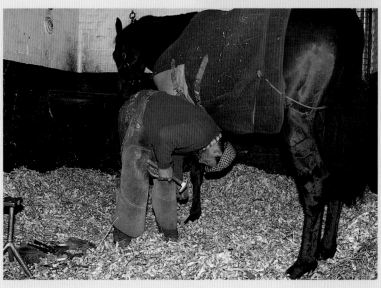

THE FARRIER

NICK FURLONG, Clive Brittain's farrier, says "I spend 90 per cent of my working life here at Clive Brittain's. My job is to make sure every horse is shod during the day so that it can go out to exercise, and to replace the shoes when necessary, usually once a month. Some people allow six shoes a month for normal exercise, as most horses wear their hind feet more quickly than their front, as that's where the power is. A horse carries its weight on its front feet, but uses the hind to propel itself.

"If a horse is doing roadwork, for example, that will require another, heavier set of shoes. Then, of course, a horse will pull shoes off when it gets excited and kicks around. The shoe's pushed back, the nails bend in the hoof and the shoe comes off.

"The shoes are mild steel, but the nails are very soft alloy as they have to be driven in and bent over. The idea is that you put a nail through the shoe into the horn. Then it's rung off, the head being twisted off, then it's risen up with the pincers and driven up to what we call a clench, and you knock the clenches over so that it's hanging into the hoof. When the horse loses a shoe you hope the shoe will come straight off and not take away part of the hoof with it, the hoof being a brittle substance.

"And horses' hooves, especially race-horses', being particularly finely bred, do deteriorate with too many shoeings. At the moment we've got one horse with a pair of glue-on shoes, because his feet are not in good condition. Glue-on shoes are not very cheap, costing about £40 for a pair, and they won't last any longer. They come in all shapes and sizes.

"During the season we go to the office every day and get the entries. Then we keep an eye on things to make sure each horse gets his aluminium racing plates the day before he runs, two days or sometimes even longer before if he's going to Scotland or abroad. We may have 600 runners a year, so it can be quite a complicated process. You have to be organized, and there's a lot of week-end work involved, often working Sundays to shoe Monday's runners.

"Racing plates come in many shapes and sizes. We use American style shoes

▲
Nick Furlong, farrier, goes about his morning's work at Clive Britain's Newmarket stables.

adapted for the British market, as extended toe grips are not allowed under Jockey Club rules. And you need small nails to go with them, as the nail isn't allowed to stand out by more than 1.5mm (1/16in) from the plate itself. The main reason for the rule is in case the horse treads on anybody, but the way I see it, if a horse is going to tread on your head he'll make a mess of it anyway, never mind what sort of shoe he's wearing.

"Some hind plates will have the heel down, in what we call a calkin, to give a bit of grip, but that's only allowed to be 6mm (1/4in) and that won't make much difference in the slippery wet anyway. And there are different weights of exercise shoe too. For the standard horse I use a certain section that adapts to most feet, and which we fit cold. We use 99 per cent machine-made shoes. I have a very wide selection, and the adaptability and quality of machine-made shoes is very good these days. If anything, they have improved the state of farriery. After all, if I made a pair of shoes for a horse and they didn't quite fit, but the horse had to go out anyway, that would be like you or I going out in a pair of boots that were too big or small. And horses get

corns too and other ailments. With machine- made shoes I can get precisely the right size by trial and error.

"Apart from my job at the stable, I also work for Newmarket Racecourse on a retainer. We go into the racecourse stables and the horseboxes the night before racing to see if there are any problems with the intented runners. Overnight we repair plates that need replacing, as some horses don't travel well. Some bad travellers will come without plates and have to be plated at the course.

"Other horses have to be shod nearer the time of the races themselves. That's not always easy. The crowds are there by then, the loud-speakers are going, the adrenalin's flowing, they've been couped up in their boxes. Then there are often problems as they're being led round the parade ring. The horse's attention is diverted towards the crowd, their head is not straight, so they're not walking straight. Or the horse walks sideways when the jockeys are about to mount, walking on the side of their feet. That's called spreading a plate. Usually we have to take the horse back to the saddling box and repair the damage.

"Then for all the Group races we go down to the start. When a trainer declares a horse to run, he ticks a form saying that if his horse loses a plate it can run without it. But some trainers will want their horses re-shod. So I either have to take off a shoe and leave it off or try to get a plate on. But it's not easy. The horse has just cantered down to the start; it's psyched up, and everything's going on around it. The commentators sometimes talk rubbish when this happens and say why can't we all get on with it. They don't seem to realize that a racehorse is a highly tuned athlete with its blood pumping round, and there it is holding one leg in the air with me trying to hammer nails into its hoof.

"All in all, in Newmarket there are about 40 farriers, including apprentices and assistants. But then there are perhaps 2500 racehorses at the peak of the season, and there are all the studs, and one stud can have many mares on it. They will each have their feet trimmed twice in 2 months and their offspring too. Most big stables retain their own farrier, but two or three smaller stables will share a farrier between them."

TRAINING

THERE IS great mystique attached to the profession (at the highest level it might be termed an art) of training racehorses. There are three essential qualities in the successful trainer: a deep love and understanding of the Thoroughbred, an intimate knowledge of horse racing and a bottomless capacity for hard work. Add to those an ability to administrate, a talent for getting on with people (necessary both in dealings with staff and with owners) and a flair for public relations, and the necessary elements required to make a good all-round trainer begin to emerge. Throughout the year, both in and out of the racing season, the weather will be one of the trainer's main preoccupations. Too much of any sort of weather and his training and racing programme can be seriously interrupted, and most trainers habitually spend a considerable amount of time examining and cursing the state of the ground.

In recent years there has been a tendency for trainers to rely more and more on technology. They now talk in terms of their horse's weight – "He's come out of the race pretty well, and only lost eleven kilos..." – and blood count. Where in the past a horse was just not himself, he is now more often than not said to be suffering from a minor blood disorder. There is a growing tendency in the largest stables to set aside a room as a laboratory where a white-coated assistant can spend many an hour peering gloomily into microscopes.

Despite all these advances, however, there is still one dreaded enemy that can't be beaten. "The virus", as it is always referred to, is an umbrella term that covers a multitude of viruses that can strike at the heart of a stable and virtually close it down for weeks or months. In the infamous case of Peter Walwyn's stable in the late 1970s, "the virus" laid the yard low for a couple of years, during which time the highly popular and much respected Walwyn fell from being an almost invincible champion to just another trainer. Sometimes the symptoms of the virus are obvious, sometimes there are no symptoms at all, and it is only a

sequence of lacklustre performances on the racecourse that makes a trainer realise his horses are below par. Some trainers, such as Henry Cecil, eschew most modern technology and claim they can tell their horses' well-being by looking at them and being with them. His incredible success does nothing to dent his claims, and the fact that Henry Cecil's stable never seems to get the virus either is almost too much for some of his disease-hit rivals to bear.

Of course, there are no hard and fast rules when it comes to training a racehorse and there are almost as many different approaches as there are trainers. To describe the average routine in the average yard is therefore an innately hazardous process, but let us throw caution to the winds and make an attempt to do precisely that.

▼
A string of horses working out during early morning gallops.

All stables, even the most laid-back, rise early, and many trainers are themselves among the first into the yard. The horses are checked and fed and then the various lots are taken onto the gallops, or into the indoor school, for various forms of exercise, and the lads get a break for a well-earned breakfast. Afterwards the horses are groomed and made comfortable for the day, and the hustle and bustle of the yard dies away at about midday to be replaced by a peace and quiet that is broken only by that most important person, the feeder, going about his business. Life returns towards the end of the afternoon when the staff return for the routine of "evening stables" and the trainer or his assistant goes from box to box feeling legs, talking to the lads and generally trying to assess the well-being of the horses.

WORK RIDERS

One of the most sought-after professionals in racing is the good work rider. When a horse is in serious training it is vital for its trainer to know as much as possible about how it is handling its routine and how close it is to fitness. A work rider of experience, judgement and sensitivity is vital to him.

In the United States, and in other countries where horses are trained on the racecourses where they will perform, much work is done against the clock. American jockeys and work riders therefore have a justified reputation for "having clocks in their heads". In England and France, riding work is a less regimented affair and trainers rely largely on the evidence of their own eyes, and on what the work riders tell them. It is no longer customary, as it was in the old days, to try horses over racing distances carrying different weights.

A horse attempting a new trip on the racecourse will usually not have been tried over the distance on the gallops either. The opinion of a good work rider is thus invaluable.

saddle, and finally to being ridden. At the same time they will acclimatize themselves to their new routine of life in a racing stable, with all the attendant noise, bustle, moments of excitement and periods of boredom.

As soon as they are ready, the yearlings will have their first taste of the training grounds. At first they will be cantered by themselves and then with other horses. They will soon learn, some sooner than others, how to fall in behind other horses or to "go upsides" and eventually perhaps how to set the pace for others to follow. When they are ready, they will be introduced to the starting stalls so that they will not be afraid of them when their big day comes.

Getting fit

After the New Year, the rate of work for the horses of all ages will be stepped up. In most stables, the majority of the inmates will be two-year-olds. There will be a good proportion of three-year-olds, now in their second season of training, and a sprinkling of older horses.

As he watches his string on the gallops, now in harder and harder work, the hawk-eyed trainer will be assessing

THE WINTER ROUTINE

THE TRAINING season begins just when the racing season is coming to an end. Most of the yearling sales take place in September and October and the trainer will be busy buying the annual quota for his owners to replace the horses in his stable that have naturally come to the end of their racing careers or have been sold out of the yard for one reason or another. Most trainers will take delivery of their new charges towards the end of November. The racing season has finished by then, so any infections brought into the yard by the new batch will be less of a threat to the stable's fortunes.

Early training

Many of the yearlings will already have been broken by the time they arrive. Those that have not will either be sent away to specialists or, more commonly, be broken in at the stable. They will slowly become used to wearing tack and

▲ *All-weather racing has proved a boon to many trainers nearer the bottom of the league, who are able to pick up small races while the big shots are taking the winter off. It also provides betting turnover on frosty days when conditions are too bad even for jump racing.*

◀ *First lot at the Kingsclere yard of Ian Balding, one of the Royal trainers.*

▶ *A Newmarket string out on the heath for some dawn air.*

A RACEHORSE'S AGE

All horses have their birthdays on New Year's Day, irrespective of when they were foaled. As they get older, the difference in their real age becomes less and less important, but in the early stages there can be a marked difference between a horse born in January and one born in June. For the record, both are officially "two-year-olds" in the New Year, but one really is almost two years old, while the other is only a year and a half. Obviously the older of the two, depending on their breeding, is likely to be stronger, or more "forward", than the other.

BREAKING IN

Yearlings usually enter the stable after the autumn sales. Most yards break them in themselves. This takes some days to achieve, though an innovatory method that takes only hours is currently gaining currency in the United States and, like all things American, may spread. Certain owners have their yearlings broken in on their studs, and there are also various places that *specialise in the art to which yearlings may be sent. Before the year is out they are learning to canter, first by themselves and then with other horses. Then in the months of January and February the young horses, now two-year olds, are put into more serious work, as the trainer begins to make an assessment of their various different abilities, temperaments and preferences.*

which of his charges are coming on best and which are lagging behind. He will often be riding out with some of the "lots" (the name given to each batch of horses as they work each morning – there are often three or four lots a day), or he will be standing by the gallops. Most stable lads will tell you that this period of winter and early spring, when they are getting the work into unfit horses, is the busiest time of their year, despite the fact that there is no actual racing. It is also customary for many flat-racing stables to keep a horse or two in training for the odd hurdle race, or, in these days of the all-weather racetracks, for the odd outing at Lingfield or Southwell, to keep up the stable interest.

Evening stables

Each afternoon, at "evening stables", the trainer will go round his horses and see how each one is faring, with particular reference to how well they are eating because this is often as good a guide as any to a horse's well-being.

He will also feel the legs of any horses that have had problems with them (a good proportion) and talk to the lads. It is remarkable just how much a good trainer will know about each of his charges. He will seem almost to be able to read each horse's mind, despite the fact that he may have 150 in his yard and the fact that, in a flat-racing stable, a horse may only be in the trainer's care for a matter of months in some cases.

THE SUMMER ROUTINE

THE FLAT RACING season proper begins at the end of March. Some trainers will have a lot of "early types" in their yards, so for them the real business begins in earnest. Others prefer to take more time with their horses and won't get into full gear until the end of April or even later. With the onset of racing, the trainer spends hours poring over the form books to decide in which races to place his horses. Then there are the owners to inform and keep happy. Some owners will take little or no interest in the yard during the close season, but as soon as they think their horse should be racing they are seldom off the telephone!

▶ *Morning exercise at Newmarket.*

In any yard, a trainer relies heavily on his staff, and in the bigger stables the trainer's role during the racing season resembles that of a general overseeing a complicated military campaign. On a busy day his horseboxes may fan out to as many as three or four courses, each box bearing horses that are trained to the minute for a particular race that suits the individual's needs and preferences. Each horse is looked after particularly carefully after each racing appearance. It is usually given a few days easy, while the trainer gauges how much or how little it has taken out of itself. Like human beings, horses vary considerably: some are tough nuts which thrive on hard work, others sensitive creatures which need to be handled as delicately as a flower.

▲ *Despite its proximity to London and increasingly suburban setting, Epsom Downs is still home to many stables.*

▶ *Lanfranco Dettori , (left) the brilliant young Italian jockey based at Newmarket, out on the gallops at Newmarket. Many consider him a possible future champion.*

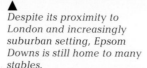

The height of the season

The season is at its busiest during the summer months, when a glut of evening race meetings adds to the stable's workload. It then winds down gradually as the days draw in to reach its conclusion at the beginning of November. The "back-end" of the season is no holiday, however. Two-year-old racing is at its peak, while trainers are also desperately scanning the *Racing Calendar* for opportunities suitable for horses which, for one reason or

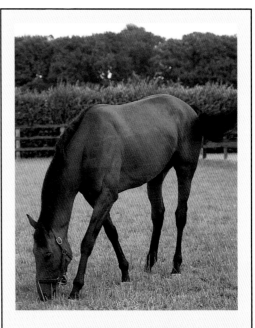

RESTING MID-SEASON

The flat season is long and arduous and it is a rare horse that can be kept on the go with consistent success. Many benefit from a mid-season break of two or three weeks, sometimes in a quiet paddock of their owner, and can then re-enter the fray with body and, just as importantly, mind refreshed. For it is a fact that some horses are psychologically tougher than others, while some are just too intelligent for their own good and think too much. The more intelligent a horse, the more he or she may suffer from the effects of a hard race or an over-long campaign. Some of the great autumn triumphs have been carried off by animals who have been lightly raced, or who have benefitted from a mid-season break. It is this sort of horse which is most likely to carry off the great end of season prize, Le Prix de L'Arc de Triomphe, while other, perhaps more able horses, are quite obviously feeling the effects of an exacting season and are left floundering in their wake.

another, they still have not been able to race. It is towards the end of the year, too, that nerves and tempers are stretched to their limit. It has been a long season.

There may have been a few triumphs, and there have certainly been disappointments. Not a few among the stable's personnel are beginning to look forward to the time when the established residents of the yard leave to take up stud or paddock duties, or more likely are transferred to another trainer to begin a career over timber, their boxes to be filled instead by an undisciplined new batch of yearlings, the subjects of hopes, dreams and fantasies for everyone from owner to stable lad during the long winter months that stretch ahead.

But there is something very exciting about the atmosphere of a successful stable when its horses are firing at the height of the season. Everybody goes about his or her work with particular zest, and there is the extra buzz of anticipation when a couple of the charges are expect to "go in" that afternoon at the big meeting.

CLIVE BRITTAIN'S APPROACH TO TRAINING

"THE BASIC secret of training is not to gallop too many times. Instead it is better to do as much long, steady work with them as you can. I often have them out in the evening and give them an hour and a half's exercise like we used to years ago when I used to ride St. Paddy out for the guv'nor (Sir Noel Murless). That was the only way you could really get him fit. He was a horse that needed to go out twice a day. (St. Paddy won the 1960 Derby and St. Leger, ridden by Lester Piggott.)

"When I get a horse I forget its breeding, however good it may be, and train its temperament instead. If it shows a bit of pace you want to make sure you're not exploiting the speed in a horse that may eventually want 1½ miles. Of course some families are easier than others. For example I know there's a problem with the

▲▲
Clive Brittain watches his string at Newmarket.

▲
Riding work at Newmarket.

◀
Clive Brittain's string returns to Carlburg stables after exercise.

Bellyphas (horses sired by Bellypha). You've had it if you let them get the better of you. They can either be over-keen, or they can switch off on you and you can't do a damn thing with them.

"We do quite a lot of the breaking-in of yearlings here, though some owners, like Sheikh Mohammed, have their horses broken elsewhere. I have a first-class staff to do the job every year. They do much of the swimming of the horses, the breaking and the stalls work. They've been together for some time, so each member of the team knows what the others are doing. That's pretty important. We take about two weeks to get a yearling broken and stalls-trained. For the stalls, they're ridden round the paddock and then they're driven in with the riders on, backed out, ridden round the paddock and then they're put back in again and the gates are shut on them.

"I was one of the first trainers to make a practice of swimming my horses in an equine pool. I've never stopped singing its praises and I think that all top-class yards should have one. Barry Hills has followed suit, and Martin Pipe came to look at mine and then put one in. Also there's the commercial one in Newmarket which is easy to use, but it has its drawbacks, including having to transport the horses there. Having one's own, you just take a horse out of its box and give it a swim.

"They either swim before exercise or after. If a horse is stiff in the morning and slow to warm up I give it eight laps and then take it out to exercise. Some horses obviously don't like swimming so I don't make them. The aim is to have a horse working for you, after all, and not to break its heart.

"To decide where to enter my horses I pick a moment when the phones aren't ringing. A quarter to five in the morning is a good time. The long-term entries we do in advance anyway, of course, but the five-day system has made the entering of horses a lot easier. When I come in from working the horse I can tick off this horse or that horse knowing that it's ready to run in the next five days if there's a suitable race. So I can work out where and when I want each horse entered. It can be quite a jigsaw puzzle. A retired Jockey Club handicapper comes in to discuss the placing of the horses twice a week, and whether they're "well in" or not.

SWIMMING

The practice of swimming horses, pioneered by Clive Brittain, is fast catching on as a method of getting or keeping a horse fit, especially one with leg problems. The principle is much the same as with human beings, and anyone who does a few lengths of a pool on a regular basis will know how the body benefits. Most horses like swimming and take kindly to the water but some don't. With the latter, as in the old adage, you can lead a horse to water but it is best not to make it swim. Lambourn-based Barry Hills and the record-breaking National Hunt Champion trainer, Martin Pipe, are among other trainers to have installed pools in their yards.

▶ *Lady Beaverbrook has for long been one of the most sporting owners on the turf, and though she has had good horses and won good races, her patience and support of the sport have never quite been rewarded in full measure. In 1991, however, she won the 2,000 Guineas with the Clive Brittain-trained Mystiko.*

"Newbury is probably my favourite course, followed by Sandown. I like Newbury because it's a fair course and because we have quite a few of our wins there, which makes it even fairer.

"Nowadays I find the all-weather racetracks (Lingfield and Southwell) an advantage. They keep the yard ticking over, and having a fit horse to work with provides a good guideline when the season proper starts.

"I get quite attached to my horses and am often sorry to see them go. Every horse has a good point, though it's damn hard to find it in some. As for me, I love racing, and I'm grateful every morning that I am in the position I am. Racing's something that I do know about, you see. In every other way I'm as thick as about ten planks."

A winning team: Steve Cauthen, Charles St. George and Henry Cecil.

◄ Henry Cecil and Sheikh Mohammed, one of the most powerful combinations in European racing.

◄ Jack Berry, the former jump jockey who by sheer hard work and not a little talent has built up his stable from humble beginnings to become one of the most formidable in the land.

TWO TRAINERS COMPARED

THE TWO leading trainers of the 1990 Flat season were Henry Cecil, in terms of prize money won, and Jack Berry, in terms of numbers of winners. The two men and their methods and stables could hardly be more different.

Henry Cecil

Henry Cecil, aristocrat and dandy, is the master of Warren Place, Newmarket, that most sumptuous of training establishments, and the undisputed master of his profession. He has weathered criticism that he was born with every possible advantage (he is the stepson of Sir Cecil Boyd-Rochfort and the former son-in-law of the late Sir Noel Murless) not only by producing an astonishing flow of Classic and Group successes, including two Derbys, but also by maintaining a strike rate, unrivalled by his contemporaries, of approximately one winner to every three runners. In 1987 he created a new record of 180 winners trained in Britain. The previous record had been established in 1846. He has also been champion trainer on nine occasions. In short, although Cecil undoubtedly has the best owners and the best horses, he also has by far the best results. He is courteous but unconventional and has an attractively relaxed approach to life, never taking himself too seriously. To make matters worse for his rivals, he often eschews many of the modern technological aids to training. Instead he consults his own instinctive feel for when a horse is right. He is nearly always right, and so nearly always are nearly all his horses.

Jack Berry

Jack Berry trains at the entirely unfashionable venue of Cockerham in Lancashire. Over the last two decades, and by sole dint of solid, hard graft, this former jump jockey has built up a stable that is now capable of producing a higher number of winners in a season than any other. This is a truly remarkable achievement for a northern stable, especially one that relies in the main on relatively inexpensive two-year-olds and which specializes in races up to 1 mile. The stable is run as a family affair, Jack's wife and sons providing a skilled and reliable back-up team. Their horses work hard for their living, but the Berrys have mastered the elusive art of keeping them on the boil throughout a long and demanding season. At the sales there is no sharper eye than Jack's. It might be said that he never buys or aims his horses too high, though when he does get an animal with a bit of quality about it, his handling of it invariably puts many a puffed-up Newmarket trainer to shame.

The different training methods of these two top stables become readily apparent with a look at the statistics. There is the old saying that comparisons are odious. In this case they are meant only to highlight the differences between two of the top stables in the land which have both reached their eminent position by completely different methods and with completely different material.

In 1990 both ran a similar number of different horses, Cecil 118 to Berry's 125, but Cecil's ran only 351 races between them to Berry's 804. Despite this discrepancy, the eventual number of winners for each stable, 111 and 127, works out at roughly the same – a win for each horse run, but Berry's horses were made to work much harder, and his overall percentage of 15.8 and level stake return of -£156.11 bear no comparison to Cecil's figures of 31.6 per cent and -£8.67.

The majority of Cecil's successes were with three-year-olds (84), while Berry was as heavily biased towards two-year-old victories (87), and while Cecil showed a marked preference for staying races,

Newmarket trainer Bill O'Gorman with his multiple winner Timeless Times.

Owner Charles St. George seen here with Geoff Potts *(left)*, head lad at Sefton Lodge.

Newmarket trainer Bill O'Gorman has made a reputation as a master handler of speed merchants and it is rare for him to enter a horse for a distance over a mile. He has had many fast winners, none more so than Timeless Times who, in 1990, equalled the long-standing record for the number of wins for a two-year old in one season with 16 victories.

It was not long ago that Bill used to put himself up on his own horses, rare on the flat, and now his daughter Emma looks likely to climb high on the tricky ladder to successful female jockeyship.

Charles St. George has owned many good horses over the years, mostly ridden by Lester Piggott in the black and white colours, including the Oaks heroine Ginevra, and the St. Leger victors Bruni and Michelozzo.

St George used to have horses in training at Findon, Sussex, with the late Ryan Price, one of the great characters of the racing scene, but now they are stabled at Sefton Lodge, Newmarket, under the supervision of Henry Cecil. St. George is still hoping to win the greatest prize of all, the Epsom Derby.

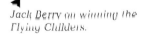

◄ *Jack Berry on winning the Flying Childers.*

with 202 of his runners performing at distances in excess of 9 furlongs, Berry's horses contested no less than 650 sprints and no more than 35 staying races.

Only 11.7 per cent of Cecil's races were handicaps, and he declined to enter his horses for even one seller. He picked up an average of £13,692 for each victory.

Of the races entered by Berry 37.4 per cent were handicaps, and he contested 124 sellers. His 127 races won were at an average of £3,128. And 31.3 per cent of Berry's races were at Group One courses, compared to 58.4 per cent of Cecil's.

It is fascinating to note the relative difference in fitness between the two stables' horses on their first outings. Only 14 of Berry's won at 11.5 per cent compared to 39 of Cecil's at 33.1 per cent.

FORM

At the very heart of racing is the study of form. Before every good race there are any number of theories about which horse will win and why. Fitness, the draw, the ground, the jockey, the trainer, the distance, and what the horses in question have achieved in the past and can be expected to achieve in the future; these are all crucial ingredients in any argument.

In recent years there has been a dramatic increase in the number of publications available to trainers and punters alike to aid them in their interpretation of form. These range from the tried and tested, through the computer-assisted mathematical, to the frankly eccentric. Some of the best information now available are the highly informative statistical breakdowns of trainers' methods and the performances of favourites and outsiders at the various different courses.

Two of the longest standing and most respected guides to the form are the Timeform Black Book *and the* Raceform Notebook. *Both are sent weekly to subscribers and soon become indispensable. The former provides summaries of each horse's past achievements and preferences and assessments of its future capabilities, together with a rating which, when compared with other horses and ratings in the same race, will provide a "best-in" in each contest. The* Raceform Notebook *supplies similar information, without a rating, in a race-by-race form, the performance of the principals in each contest being analysed in greater or lesser detail, and pointers to future runnings being given. Both organizations employ the best race-readers in the business.*

PLANNING A PROGRAMME

YOU HAVE a wonderful horse that is trained to the minute in an almost perfect stable. Now you have to decide where and when to race him. This is an aspect of the racing game that should never be dismissed lightly. There is a bewildering array of races in the calendar spread over a large number of racecourses, all with their own quirks. However brilliant your horse, there is no point in entering him in a 11 mile race at Ascot when it is clear that he barely stays 7 furlongs and has a decided left-handed bias. Then there is always the ground to be considered. While it is a commonly stated claim that a good horse will act on any going, it is also the case that most horses prefer one sort of ground to another and need the surface of their preference to produce their best form.

All these matters, and many more besides, must be taken into account by the trainer and owner when entering their horse for the races, and it is clear that some trainers are far more astute than others in this field. Some trainers are famous for the clever placing of their horses. Others run their animals in such hopelessly ill-suited events that all sorts of motives are attributed to them other than that of trying to win. Some of the bigger stables now sensibly have a part- or even full-time race planner on the staff, combing the formbooks and the handicap ratings to find the right races. And with the growing internationalism of

▼ *Out of the stalls at Lingfield.*

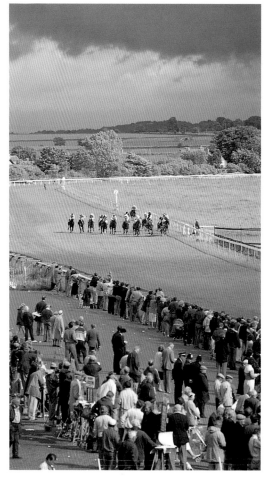

racing, there are not only the British races to peruse, but also those of many other countries. Trainers like John Dunlop, Ian Balding, Paul Cole, Clive Brittain and others have been setting an example of highly successful foreign raiding for some years, and many other trainers are now following suit.

Placing a horse can be one of the most enjoyable parts of the training process,

▲
Newmarket dawn.

◀
Bath is an attractive upland track where the quality of the racing may be modest but is always entertaining.

▼
Taking a tight turn at Chester.

and it has been made a good deal simpler by the relatively new five-day system. A horse is entered for a race five days before the event, and then declared a definite runner or absentee by 10 a.m. on the morning before (this system applies to all but the biggest races). Let us then map out a programme for a typical, average racehorse in an imaginary couple of seasons.

PLANNING A PROGRAMME – THE DEBUT

OUR HORSE is a nice, if unfashionably-bred colt which we have put into training with a reliable handler based in the Midlands. The colt is related to a couple of two-year-old winners, so there is every reason to hope that it might also pick up a race in its first season. We are delighted to hear from the trainer on the first Monday in June that the colt has come to hand and that it is time to be thinking about its debut. It is thought that he might not be quite fast enough to win at the minimum distance, so we decide to look for a small maiden race over 6 furlongs at one of the Midland tracks, in order to cut out unnecessary travelling.

At first we are frustrated. There are 5-furlong two-year-old races. There is a selling race over 6 at a local track, and there are suitable-looking races in the south and north, but there is nothing to suit us. Indeed, it transpires that if we want to run our colt before the end of the month, and we do, only one race will suffice, a small 6-furlong two-year old maiden for colts and geldings at Nottingham on Tuesday June 28th, worth a mere £2,056 to the winner. We begin to feel sympathy for all those trainers who complain about the lack of opportunities for their charges. If it is this difficult finding the sort of race we are looking for, imagine the problems if you have a four-year-old filly who won't stay a yard over 7 furlongs, and who has been given too much weight to run in handicaps but isn't quite up to Listed or Group class.

Nottingham is a flat, easy track and a good one for introducing juveniles. Indeed, the likes of Henry Cecil often use it for this purpose (the great Triple Crown winner Oh So Sharp made her debut here), and there is always the

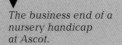

▼ *The business end of a nursery handicap at Ascot.*

worry that a modest maiden may include some very decent animals. Anyway, we enter our colt on the previous Thursday. The next day we excitedly turn to the racing daily to find our horse's name listed in alphabetical order for the particular race under Tuesday's entries. In Saturday's paper he appears again, this time with a weight – 9st – allotted to him. This race is simple. All colts are to carry 9st, and geldings 8st 11lb. On Monday the trainer declares the horse a runner, and we note with satisfaction that the advance going is "good". We can't complain about that. The yard does not retain a jockey, and we decide to book a locally-based man who has ridden our horse in his work a couple of times. So on Tuesday morning, horse and connections duly turn up at Nottingham racecourse, full of anticipation.

The going is indeed good, and there are 21 other runners, many having their first outing and some having run before. The colt looks good in the paddock and our trainer is well thought of, so he goes down to the post not entirely unfancied at 14/l. He is quite well drawn at 15, the stalls being on the stands' side and high numbers therefore being considered to have an advantage over Nottingham's straight 6 furlongs. There is a slight mist, and we cannot see much of the start. When they are 1 mile out it is clear that he is running an excellent race and is up with the leaders. Then quite suddenly he seems to run out of steam. The jockey is sensibly not hard on him when his chance has gone, and he finishes "out with the washing" in about fifteenth position.

The winner's time is slow, and there is nothing in the field that appears to be out

of the ordinary. Nevertheless we are delighted with the run, and the jockey tells us that the horse "blew up approaching the last". Over the next few days, having found out that the horse has recovered well from the run, we decide to look for a similar race about three weeks after the first. We are convinced that he did not last out the 6 furlongs through lack of fitness rather than lack of potential stamina, and the trainer tells us he is bound to come on for the race.

GEOFF LEWIS

Geoff Lewis was for many years one of Britain's leading jockeys, and his name will always be particularly associated with Mill Reef, with whom he set up a thrilling partnership that only had its colours lowered once in his career, and took in the Derby, the King George VI and Queen Elizabeth Diamond Stakes and Le Prix de L'Arc de Triomphe on its road to immortality. Geoff was also first jockey to Noel Murless, debatably the greatest trainer of the post-war era. He himself now trains with some success at Epsom and is one of the most liked and respected figures in racing.

▲
A hard fought maiden at Goodwood.

THE FOLLOW UP

The second outing

Again we find it hard to pick a suitable race and are forced to wait until Monday July 25th, almost a month after the debut, when Nottingham again comes to our rescue with an evening meeting that includes a 6-furlong event for maiden two-year-olds and a prize of £2,868. Even at the five-day stage it is clear that this is going to be a popular race, and on the day before we learn that it has been divided in order to meet Nottingham's safety limit, our colt being balloted to run in Division Two.

This time the going is good to soft and we are drawn nine of sixteen. The same jockey as before is booked to ride. We think that a little too much use might have been made of him last time out, and he is told to lie handy and come with a run no earlier than the 2-furlong pole. The trainer is hopeful and so are we, and the colt goes off at 8/l, having opened at 6s and then drifted as far as 12s before attracting support. The race goes like a

dream. Seeming to like the rain-softened ground, he starts a run about 2 furlongs out and, responding to his rider's efforts, gets up to catch the leader for a thrilling dead-heat in the closing strides, looking like he would stay further. The time is unimpressive, at 8.3 seconds below standard. Our share of the spoils amount to only £717, but the sheer pleasure and excitement are worth many thousands.

The third outing

Once again the colt seems to come out of the race well. The plan is now to strike while the iron is hot and go for a slightly better race over another furlong or two, it looking pretty certain that he will stay the extra distance, within the next fortnight. We would now be prepared to travel further if necessary, his two little trips to Nottingham having caused no problem, and we certainly would not fear soft ground.

Again we have difficulties finding a race. All the 7 furlong races for two-year-olds are "nurseries", or handicaps, for which we feel our horse is not yet quite ready, and the first suitable races both fall on Thursday 11th August at Salisbury and Yarmouth, a little later than we had hoped. At the five-day stage we enter for both, our preference being for the Salisbury contest. Salisbury's 7 furlongs are stiffer than Yarmouth's, and we think that will be in our favour. Also, at £3,250, it is worth almost £1,000 more. At the overnight stage the advance going is fast ground for Yarmouth and good for Salisbury. That decides us, and we declare for the Salisbury contest.

Meanwhile, the horse we dead-heated with in the last race has appeared again, only a week later, over 7 furlongs at Wolverhampton, where he has run a very distant fourth on firm ground that may have been against him. Even so, the form

▼ *A close finish in a graduation stakes at Bath.*

of "our" race has hardly been boosted. Moreover, our regular jockey is unable to make the trip to Salisbury, but we are lucky enough to book one of the top riders in the country, the retained jockey for a powerful Sussex yard, so there are no worries on that score. The favourite is a hotpot previous winner from a big Lambourn stable, and our colt, conceding, like the favourite, 5lb to the maidens of the race, goes off at a generous looking 10/1.

The price looks less generous a few minutes later when the hotpot wins a shade comfortably with our colt 5 and a half lengths back in sixth. There are no excuses. Always chasing the leaders, we had every chance but just ran on at one pace in the last 2 furlongs. It seems that we just came up against better horses on the day, and the only niggling suspicion remaining to us is that our horse may well be a soft-ground specialist. Yet again he comes out of the race well, but we decide with our trainer to give him a bit of an easy, then bring him back for a couple of nurseries over 7 furlongs or 1 mile towards the end of the season when

▲ *Pat Eddery and Gary Bardwell at work at Ascot.*

the ground may have eased. In the interim, the Salisbury hotpot runs in a decent two-year-old contest at Goodwood, starts favourite again and is a respectable fourth. It is clear that our colt is no world-beater and we decide to keep our sights fairly low.

LATE SEASON

IT IS TOWARDS the end of September when he is ready for his next outing. The summer weather has remained fine and the ground has not eased, though there has been a little rain in the far north. Suddenly a race presents itself. It is a small nursery at Edinburgh over a mile on Monday 3rd October and there is the prospect of ground to suit us. It is a long way to travel, but the season is running out and we are anxious to have a go. We enter, are given a surprisingly light weight (we are not sure whether to be delighted or insulted) and when the forecast is for good to soft going, we declare.

The race is worth £1,988 to the winner. The mile at Edinburgh involves a sharp right-hand turn into the home straight,

something our colt has not tackled before, but is otherwise undemanding. Neither of our previous two jockeys are available, and we book a northern-based lightweight able to ride at our allotted 7st 13lb. He is told to stay handily placed and come with a run about ¼ mile out. We are drawn in midfield of 14 runners and, hopes being high, we are not entirely surprised to find ourselves sent off at 9/2 joint favourite.

In the event we suffer a grave disappointment. The colt is already being ridden to hold his pitch as they turn into the straight and has nothing more to offer as the contest develops in the last ¼ mile. We eventually finish fifth, over 11 lengths behind the winner, who was giving us 5lb.

It is possible that the colt was not fully race-fit, but another explanation is beginning to look more apt – that he is just plain slow. More and more, it looks as if the Nottingham dead-heat was one of those lucky flukes. It certainly seems as though he may need an even longer trip, but we know that nurseries over more than a mile simply do not exist and we decide to put him away for the season,

▲
Racing in Florida.

▼
Further Flight (right) *wins the Ebor Handicap at York.*

bring him back into work after Christmas and give him his first outing as a three-year-old over 1¼ miles as soon as possible, while there is still a chance of the soft ground that we think he prefers.

The winter months are always frustrating. Patience, never a strong point perhaps, is stretched to the limit. But there is at least the chance to thumb the fixtures list and dream of impossible victories.

THE SECOND SEASON

THE COLT winters well. We find what appears on paper to be the ideal opportunity at our favourite Nottingham on Monday 11th April, an unusual sort of event over 1¼ miles for three-year-olds that have not won more than one race. The ground is good to soft. We have the same course and conditions that gave us our only success. None of our former riders are available, so we book a reliable jockey, refrain from giving him orders, and hope for the best. We are set to carry 8st 8lb, receiving over 1st from the odds-on favourite, a horse from a big Newmarket yard who won an important race as a two-year-old but has disappointed since. It disappoints again, running like a pig.

Our colt, on the other hand, comes up trumps. Beginning a move entering the straight, he maintains his run, leads at the distance and wins by 2½ lengths going away, having drifted in the market

▶ *Tack room and stable yard.*

▼ *Old Vic* (nearside) *and Michelozzo, two of the brightest stars in Henry Cecil's galaxy, take exercise.*

from 8s to 12s. The prize money is a much-needed £1,666. Seen in the paddock, he looks slightly in need of the outing, and normally we could expect further improvement. I say "normally" because quite frankly we no longer know what to expect. It seems clear, however, that the colt likes a trip, and we decide to go for broke and enter him for a better sort of race over an extra 2 furlongs in about three week's time. It is also clear that, for whatever reason, he loves Nottingham, and that a left-handed, flat surface with easy bends holds no terror for him. Looking back to the Edinburgh race of last season, a possible explantion is that the right-handed, sharp turn was not to his liking.

It is not in fact until Saturday 14th May that we race again. This time we decide upon a good three-year-old handicap, worth over £4,000 to the winner, over 1¼ miles at Newbury, where the ground promises to be soft. Newbury is admittedly a left-handed track, but it is also the first Group One course we have visited. Yet we decide we can't wait for ever. We are in with a good racing weight of 8st 8lb and the horse seems tremendously well. The jockey who served us so well last time is available again, and we have the pleasure of seeing our colours go down to the start on this magnificent track in front of a huge Saturday crowd. Neither are we disgraced. The winner, carrying a mere 7st 6lb, strikes the front fully 3 furlongs out and never looks likely to be caught. We move up steadily to take second place below the distance and can make little impression on him. We still finish a good two lengths in front of the third of the nine runners, and collect a useful second prize.

And so the season goes on. We next fly a little too high with an abortive but very

▲
Nobody works harder, with more enthusiasm and for so little reward than the dedicated stable lad. Why? Because he loves horses.

◄
Dowsing wins the Vernons Sprint Cup at Haydock Park.

exciting trip for a rich 1½ mile handicap at Ascot, coming sixth. Then the colt is given a break. We bring him back for two more races, both over 1¾ miles and neither successful, before selling him at the end of the season to go hurdling. The two wins gained by our imaginary horse are rather more than we could justifiably expect. Otherwise this sort of career shows the fun and importance of race planning for a horse even of our colt's mediocrity.

Different trainers approach the tricky business of race-planning from widely differing angles, and an in depth study of the methods of an acknowledged master of the art, Luca Cumani for example, can be very rewarding. Indeed, the computer age has produced a whole clutch of publications which break down stable statistics into minute detail never previously available to the public.

It is certainly the case that in every race, be it a humble handicap at Hamilton or the Derby itself, there are several horses which should not be in it, unsuited by course, distance, ground or some other factor. There is also nearly always at least one horse which is ideally suited to the contest in most aspects and, as long as he is fit, that is the horse to be on.

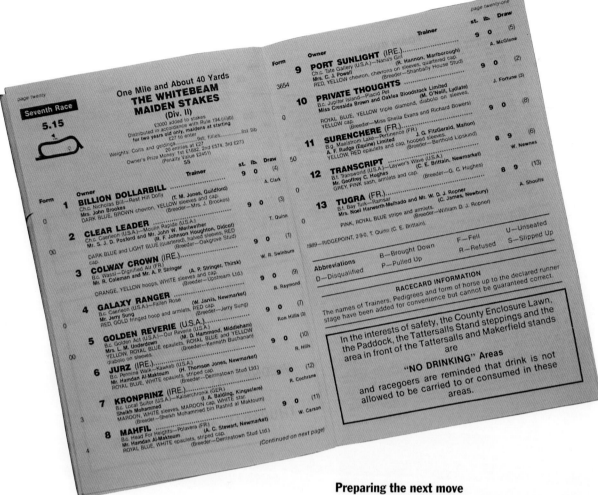

The racecard for Transcript's second outing.

TRANSCRIPT'S EARLY TESTS

TRANSCRIPT'S first outing was not a success. She had been entered at an evening meeting at Nottingham on 6th August in a race for maiden two-year-olds over 6 furlongs and worth a paltry £2,659 to the winner. The bookmakers put her in the market at 12/1 but eventually let her drift out to 20s, a price that reflected the lack of confidence behind her. Ridden by Michael Roberts, she soon showed that her price, if anything, was cramped. Always outpaced, she finished eleventh of twelve and tailed off behind Luca Cumani's Gracebridge. It was agreed after the contest that she not only needed the run (Clive Brittain's horses almost always strip a good deal fitter after their first race, which they seldom win) but also hated the fast ground. It was decided to wait until the rains came before risking her again, and despite the disappointment of this first run, Clive had a hunch, an instinct, that Transcript was much better than that.

▲
The racecard for Transcript's second outing.

▶
The number board.

▶▶
Billy Newnes (right) and Ray Cochrane (left) at Haydock.

Preparing the next move

As it was, the country continued to bask in continual sunshine and all Transcript's connections could do was sit and wait, flicking the pages of the calendar in frustration as summer turned to autumn and the racing season took on that "back-end" look that signals it is drawing gradually to a close.

Then at last the weather broke, and as there was more rain in the north than the south, Clive Brittain in Newmarket began to keep an eye out for an opportunity on the far side of the Trent, bearing in mind that he had decided she could now do with a bit more than the 6 furlongs she had previously raced over. He eventually entered the filly for a choice of two tiny races at Haydock Park, where the ground was forecast as "soft", on the 10th and 11th of October.

In the morning of the 9th, having studied the opposition in both races, he gave his instructions to his secretary, Karen Saunders, who declared Transcript a runner for the Whitebeam Maiden Stakes for two-year-olds over 1 mile and 40 yd on Wednesday 10th October.

Transcript's second outing

The filly travelled up from Newmarket the night before in a consignment of half-a-dozen horses from Carlburg Stables entered to run at the two-day Haydock meeting. She had spent the night comfortably enough in the racecourse stables and seemed to be in good heart. Sue Davidson, Clive Brittain's second travelling head lad, was in charge of operations, with two other lads. Clive himself was at the sales in Ireland, while Transcript's owner had understandably declined to make the journey north.

Confidence was not high among Transcript's connections. "She won't mind the ground", which was like a bog, was the most positive of remarks that could be elicited from Sue Davidson, and it was agreed in general that, after an absence from the course of 64 days, Transcript was bound to need the run.

Transcript was saddled up in the racecourse stables and led into the pre-parade ring to walk around and loosen her joints. Then it was time for the runners to enter the paddock proper, followed by a desultory group of connections who huddled in the rain under the partial protection of a couple of trees.

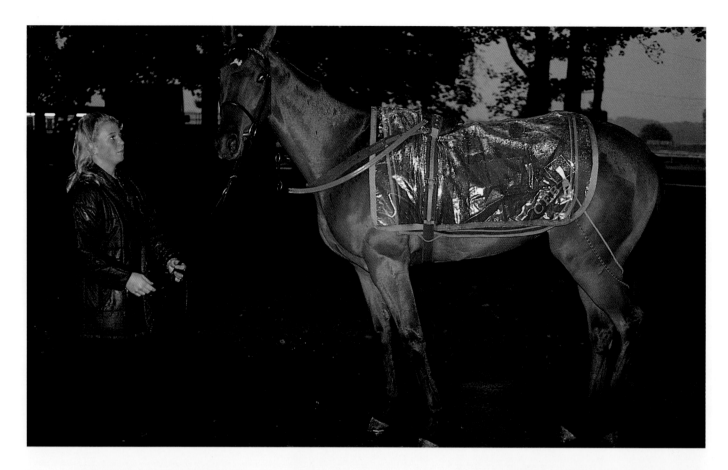

TRANSCRIPT'S NEAR SUCCESS

IT WASN'T quite the Derby and the bookmakers weren't exactly knocked off their boxes in the rush to "get on". There was some money for the first three in the betting, a decent £1,200 each-way bet on Jurz being the largest recorded. Transcript, with no confidence behind her, was friendless in the market, being put in at 20/1 and being allowed to drift out to 33s, with only two forlorn 50/1 shots to save her from the ignominy of being the least fancied horse in the race.

The 1 mile and 40 yd start at Haydock is on the opposite side of the course from the stands. The horses run left-handed into and round the last bend and then level up for the 4½-furlong run-in. Transcript went sweetly into stall six. Drawn in mid-field, there could be no excuses on that score. Neither could there be in terms of weight. She was carrying 8st 9lb, receiving, like the other two fillies in the race, a sex allowance of 5lb from the colts. Billy Newnes' (Transcript's jockey on this outing) riding weight was 8st 3lb, so Transcript was carrying only 6lb of "dead" weight (lead) under her saddle.

▲
Transcript, the apple of our eye.

▼
A mud-spattered Billy Newnes brings Transcript home in second place at Haydock.

It took 1 minute 55.19 seconds to run the extended mile at Haydock, 14.29 seconds slower than the standard, or average, due to the appalling conditions. The stalls opened at 5.20 – five minutes late – to a fairly level break, though Jurz, the second favourite, and Billion Dollarbill, one of the 50/1 shots, were rather slowly into their stride. Colway Crown cut out the early pace, heading a group comprising Port Sunlight, Surenchere, Mahfil,

Private Thoughts, Tugra and Galaxy Ranger, all these soon joined by Jurz. Transcript was towards the rear of the field as they raced down the back straight and swung round the bend towards the run-in.

There is a critical moment in every race. In the Whitebeam Maiden Stakes (Div. II) this moment came about 2½ furlongs from the line. It was then that the long-time leader Colway Crown began to tire very rapidly and was headed by Jurz. At the same time Tugra, Private Thoughts and Galaxy Ranger began putting out distress signals, though Mahfil, Surenchere and Port Sunlight were still in contention. Most importantly, the favourite Kronprinz and Transcript began making good progress towards the leading group.

In another 100 yards the position had changed again. After a brief moment of glory, Jurz yielded first place to Surenchere and began to fall away. Transcript was running the legs off the favourite and, making smooth progress

▲
Being led in.

▼
All smiles in the unsaddling enclosure.

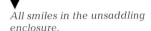

through the leaders, she hit the front approaching the final furlong. This was now a race indeed, and it looked as if Transcript was going to win it. But Tony McGlone on Port Sunlight thought differently and, asking his mount the vital question, he took up the lead inside the last 200 yards and ran on well through the mud to beat Transcript by 1½ lengths, with Surenchere another 1½ lengths back in third.

To the world in general, Transcript's second in a modest maiden at Haydock

► *Clever girl.*

Park was a matter of great unimportance, but it must be remembered that over half the horses racing each season do not manage to get into the first three in any of their races. It is not the Mill Reefs and Dancing Braves who are truly representative of horse racing, but the unsung maidens racing for a prize of £2,461 on a dismal, wet afternoon at Haydock.

Transcript had run an excellent race and had confirmed Clive Brittain's judgement that she had a certain something about her. Now it was a question of seeing how she came out of what must have been a tiring slog through the mud. Perhaps it would be possible to get another race into her before the season's end. Perhaps a maiden fillies' race over 7 furlongs might suit her ideally. As it turned out, this was to be her last outing of the season.

AT THE RACES

THE RACES

WHEN ALL is said and done, it is to the races that all roads finally lead. However good a horse's pedigree may seem on paper, however brilliant he may appear to be on the gallops, all is as naught unless the animal can fulfill expectations on the racecourse. And it is on the racecourse, often only on the racecourse, that most followers of racing come into contact with the horses, jockeys, lads and all the personnel of racing, and most of us arrive, enjoy ourselves and leave without much thought to the huge amount of organization that goes into making a day at the races.

Getting to the course

Depending on how far they have to travel (runners at far-off courses will have left the day before), the horses with racing engagements will set off for the track on the morning of the race. The travelling head lad will be in charge of their preparations and journey. It is his or her responsibility to make sure all the necessary equipment, including the colours of the relevant owners, are put safely in car or horsebox, and his or her responsibility too to supervize the safe loading of the horses into the horsebox. The horses themselves will most likely have done no more than an exercise walk or trot that morning. Some travel better than others, and they all require varying degrees of attention. In most cases their own particular lad will be travelling with them. When they get to the course the horses will be unloaded and installed in one of the course boxes in the stable area to which unauthorized persons are strictly refused admission.

As well as all the horseboxes that will be leaving yards all over the country to converge upon the racecourse, there will also be a small army of other professionals heading in the same direction – officials, valets, pressmen, jockeys, traders, catering staff, trainers, and owners. Every day hundreds of men and women who depend upon racing for their living leave home for one of the many courses

▲
Apprentices at Sha Tin racecourse, Hong Kong.

scattered over the length and breadth of the country. There is even a man who produces different-coloured number cloths for the television racing teams. There are many supporters of the game who would be loth to lose the smaller courses, thus detracting from the variety of the sport, but many of the professionals would be only too glad not to have to travel long distances for one-day meetings of little importance at obscure and far-flung courses.

DEBORAH KAYNE

Deborah Kayne is the Assistant and Secretary to the Clerk of the course at Lingfield Park, Surrey. Her duties include acting as the Clerk of the Course when the Clerk is away on other duties. She also makes a regular tour of the ground to check on the daily duties of the groundstaff.

There have only ever been three women who have held a license to act as the Clerk and she is the youngest to hold the post. She combines the full time job of helping to run the day-to-day activities of the course which now has more than 60 race days in a year, with that of mother of a young baby and general home duties.

A Day at the Races

In times gone by there was more camaraderie in racing. In the days before motorways and private planes a small army of professionals and hangers-on would arrive in a town, Chester for example, for a few days racing. Each night the hotels and bars would be full of talk of the day's sport and the prospects for tomorrow, and jockeys and trainers would be rubbing shoulders with pressmen, owners and professional gamblers.

Yet now, in the hard-nosed, commercial, modern world, and with the great advances in the ease and speed of travel, a jockey or trainer will want to be back in Newmarket or Lambourn each night, ready to ride out or supervise his string early the next morning. And with the advent of Satellite Information Services and the excellent coverage of the major meetings by the BBC and Channel 4, there is little need for the hard-worked trainer to attend a meeting at all if he is not inclined to.

Nevertheless, there is nothing quite like a day at the races to get a feel of the sport, and for those who have never done so, it is well worth arriving at a course - and a small mid-week meeting can be just as rewarding as the packed-out big occasion - two or three hours before the first race, when the track is only inhabited by the professionals who need to get there early. It is fun to stroll about and watch as people slowly drift in from all over the country - the officials, the trainers, the horses, the press and the jockeys, and the atmosphere slowly builds up to the time of the off for the first.

◄
Head Groundsman, Paul Deacon, who is responsible for the complete upkeep of the course and enclosures, oversees groundsman Sean McLaughlin who is testing the depth of the Equitrack, the all-weather course at Lingfield Park.

►
Security Stables Manager, Bill Sutton, cleans out each stall after a meeting. Here he is seen using a Terra-vac which sucks all waste material efficiently up and into a trailer container behind the tractor.

THE CLERK OF THE COURSE

THE OFFICIAL responsible for the running of the racecourse is the Clerk of the Course. His tasks are numerous and varied, from the maintenance and improvement of the buildings themselves, to the framing of races and the smooth operation of racedays. Many Clerks have made great names for themselves, especially those who have recognized the necessity of selling racing to the public in the modern age. They have also moved into the area of marketing. Many racetracks are used for activities other than racing and the hiring out of buildings for conferences and functions, outside of racedays, can be more profitable than the actual racing itself. The Clerk also has to be an expert public relations man. Corporate entertaining has become big business, and the sponsorship of races, even the Classics, is now essential to the well-being of the sport.

Captain Nick Lees is Chief Executive and Clerk of the Course at Newmarket, Britain's premier racetrack. He is in evidence everywhere at Newmarket, and seems to have the knack of being in three different places at the same time. He rightly insists that Newmarket is more than just a racecourse – or two racecourses as it happens. It is a business. He has an office staff of nine, including a Company Secretary, an accountant and a Racecourse Manager, and there are 30 other people on a payroll that stretches to a head groundsman, three gardeners, two painters, a bricklayer, an electrician, a plumber and a blacksmith. As Clerk of the Course he is also particularly responsible for the condition of the racecourse itself and the cultivation of the ground. He has to make sure that the surface is right and that the running rails are in good repair.

Sponsorship is one of his main preoccupations. He has to get as much as he can. In 1991 Newmarket offered £3.2 million in prize money spread over 31 days' racing, of which £1.3 million came from commercial sponsors. This was no mean achievement, especially as racing has to take its place in an ever-growing line of spectator sports and other activities queuing up for support.

Much of the prize money is put up by the racecourse itself.

▲
Captain Nick Lees, Clerk of the Course, in the weighing room at Newmarket.

"Admissions play a vital part in the prize money," says Captain Lees. "Racecourses abroad, of course, get their money from betting, but because of the system in Britain we have to get it from admissions. That's why it's so very expensive to get into a British racecourse." (Entry into the first, Craven, meeting at Newmarket in 1991 stood at £12 for day members and £8 for Tattersalls.)

The racecourse also earns money from other sources. There are contracts with television and with Satellite Information Services, both important supplies of funding. Then there are any number of activities in between race meetings: conferences, antiques fairs, dog shows, dinners and discotheques, though Newmarket does less well in this respect than some courses, which earn more money from non-racing activities than they do from racing itself. Newmarket is surrounded by 2,500 horses in training and

▲ *Newmarket has two different courses and two sets of stands. Here, horses approach the finish on the July course, used only in the summer months.*

hundreds of acres of gallops, and, as Lees puts it, "Horses and people don't always go together."

Framing Races

The framing of races is an area that could be improved on certain courses, which seem to have a perennial struggle in trying to attract runners. Newmarket and Nick Lees have no such problems. In the average week he has no need to consider race conditions at all, and he puts his mind to them for only two or three sessions annually, particularly during September and October when he applies his attention to the next year's racing. Newmarket has evolved a highly successful pattern of racing over the years, and Lees finds it necessary to change, to a greater or lesser extent, only 10 to 20 races a year. He has gradually cut out a batch of two-year-old races in the spring, for example, because they simply were

not filling. On the other hand, during his 19 years at Newmarket he has seen various races grow in stature or change in nature. The Newmarket executive has invented two Pattern races, for instance, the Rockfel Stakes and the Van Geest Criterion Stakes, and other races replace those that were not going so well.

NEWMARKET'S TWO COURSES

Newmarket is unique in having two racecourses. Lees admits that on economic grounds this is not an ideal situation. "The July course is extremely popular" he points out. "It is also very easy to run. It is a simple racecourse, in its structure rather like a minor league racecourse. There is no heating or escalators, and it takes very little to maintain. Most importantly, the public love it, and we get good crowds. In fact, the course would take more than the 13 days a year it is currently allotted."

The Rowley Mile course, on the other hand, is used for eight days in the spring and ten in the autumn, and it wouldn't take much more. Between November and the spring very little grass grows and the executive only gets away with the amount of racing held on it by dividing the course. In the spring they race on the stands' side course, and in the autumn on the far side. In a wet autumn the far side ground can be badly chopped up, and the grass does not grow in time for the opening Craven meeting. These are all problems that a Clerk of the Course has to deal with.

Looking after a turf course

The ground at Newmarket is famously good. "There is no drainage here," says Lees, "God does the lot. There is only 9 to 18 inches of topsoil, and under that is pure white chalk. It drains beautifully and is lovely, light land, which is partly why Newmarket became what it is."

On the controversial subject of watering courses, Lees is illuminating. "By having two courses we are able to preserve the ground in more ways than one. On the Rowley Mile, however dry it is in the summer we just leave it, and let nature take its course. The roots of the grass have to go down and down to find the water, and in doing so the turf retains its character. Many racecourses in Britain and France have been knackered by over-watering. In those circumstances only rye grass survives, and all the old, tough, coarse heath grasses disappear. We hardly ever put weedkiller on Newmarket because we encourage resilient herbage."

He has every sympathy, however, for all those Clerks at racecourses that are naturally less well-endowed than Newmarket. Many Clerks are constantly having to make invidious decisions about whether to water the turf or not. If they do, it invariably begins to rain and then they are left with a quagmire. If they don't, then trainer after trainer begin to pull out their horses because of the firm ground. Nevertheless, Lees points to Carlisle and Bath as examples of courses that are never watered. The going can become very firm, but the grass provides a good cover, and the ground suits a variety of horses. Neither course lacks runners.

▼
Horses flash past the stands on Newmarket's Rowley Mile Course, scene of the first two Classics of the season, the 1,000 and 2,000 Guineas.

Raceday

On one of his many racedays, Lees reaches the course at about 8 o'clock, having rung the media on the way to inform them of the weather and the going. (Unlike some less fortunate Clerks, he does not have to worry too much about either. A raceday at Newmarket was last abandoned in 1908, when freak gales blew down all the tents and the running rails).

First he walks round the course and makes sure everything is all right. Nine million pounds has been spent at Newmarket in the last six years and he expects the best. Then he goes to his office until 10, where the phone is redhot with calls from trainers, foreign visitors and the usual clutch of people thinking that they should be allowed in for free. After he has dealt with this business, he comes down to his other office in the weighing-room, sees his staff, and fills in a few forms. Then he makes a point of walking round every bar and catering outlet to make sure they are all clean and up to scratch. From then on he is always in evidence, always at someone's beck and call.

RACECOURSE MANAGER

Newmarket is a big enough course to need to employ a racecourse manager, Chris Kennedy, though on many courses this job would be rolled into one with that of Clerk of the Course. Chris is very much involved with the marketing and corporate entertainment side of the business. He spends much of his time trying to sell the racecourse for conferences, exhibitions and trade fairs. And with the racecourse foreman he has responsibility, too, for the maintenance and tidiness of the course.

As with the Forth Bridge, there is a continuous painting programme in operation. There are also 101 separate stables, or boxes, at Newmarket that come under his jurisdiction. They are particularly busy at the Guineas meetings and at the popular evening meetings.

On racedays he is in the front line when it comes to problems with the public, and he arrives at the course early and leaves late. It was Newmarket that unluckily "copped the big one" in terms of the modern phenomenon of crowd violence when a man was killed in a drunken brawl after the last on the July course a few years ago. Though usually the course has few problems in this area, this horrendous event necessitated the spending of £30,000 on extra security.

Chris also oversees the growing trend towards corporate hospitality that is such an important part of the modern racecourse's income. On One Thousand Guineas day in 1990 the racecourse dealt with 3500 hospitality covers. On an ordinary day's racing there are 8-10,000 admissions, and this swells to 18-20,000 for a big race. Some 12,000 come to the evening meetings, including a large influx from London.

THE JUDGE

MICHAEL HANCOCK is the Jockey Club's Senior Judge. His family have been connected with racing for more than 100 years. He spends his day ascending to and descending from the judge's box perched high above the racecourse, from where he calls the all-important finishing order of the first four horses or, if there is any doubt, issues the announcement "Photograph", denoting a photo-finish. It is then that the public spend an agonizing few minutes while the photofinish film is developed in amazingly fast time and put on the judge's screen for him to decide the winner.

It is from the same photostrip that he decides upon the extended finishing order and distances separating all the runners at the finish. The same photostrip gives him the automatically calculated time of the race. The photofinish was introduced shortly after the World War II and has been progressively refined ever since, the latest innovation being the introduction of colour. It is extremely accurate and never has to be enlarged.

The judge needs to have an extensive knowledge of racing colours, be a very competent race-reader, and possess an unflappable temperament. Sometimes he

▲
Perched up on high in his eyrie, up several flights of stairs, the Judge necessarily has one of the best views on the course.

▼
Technicians with photo-finish equipment occupy the vantage point adjacent to the Judge's box.

will have to work under great pressure, especially if there is a big field and bad conditions. He cannot afford to make a mistake. He does not have an assistant, but he works with an announcer whose job it is to let the public know the result. From the judge's professional point of view some racecourses are more difficult than others. The straight course at

Kempton, which is laid diagonally across the track, has a notoriously awkward finishing angle. Ascot, on the other hand, is the judge's perfect course, as his box is at exactly the right optical point in relation to the winning-post.

Michael Hancock works a five-day week and officiates at most of the principal racecourses. As usual, travelling is the main bugbear. In his case, there is the added stress involved in always driving against the clock. After all, what on earth would happen if the judge didn't turn up?

Indeed, it is precisely that question that occasionally preys on Michael Hancock's mind. He has a recurring nightmare that haunts him when he is ill that the horses are running and he can't find the way to the judge's box in time to see them pass the post. Luckily for all, this has never happened in reality.

▶
Michael Hancock, Judge, watches the action at Newmarket's Craven meeting.

▼
Two horses strive to get their noses first past the finishing line. A mirror image helps the Judge to reach his verdict – in this case, a short head in favour of number five.

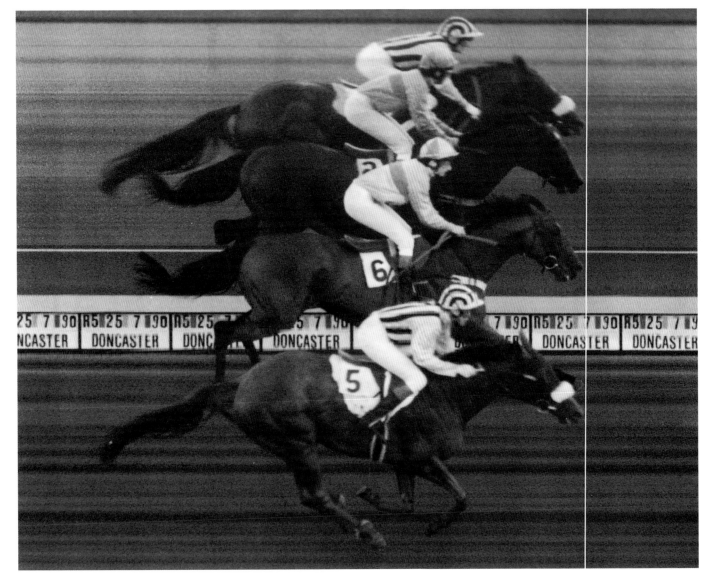

THE STEWARD'S SECRETARY

MAJOR PETER STEVENEY is the senior Stewards' Secretary. His job is to see that racing is run under the Rules, that it is safe, and that the punters get a fair deal. Each day before racing he gets together with the Handicapper and the Betting Intelligence Officer. Together they build a picture of how they expect each race to be run. The Stewards' Secretary is aided by having a file on many of the horses and copious notes on their past form and history, whether they have behaved in an unruly or wayward manner, whether they were tenderly ridden last time out or perhaps badly hampered. There may be certain aspects in maiden races that the Stewards are particularly interested in monitoring.

The Stewards are then briefed on the results of this meeting. The point of all this is to watch out during the racing for unexpected developments and results that will most likely be perfectly reasonable and above board, but which just might become the subject of a Stewards' Enquiry. On British racecourses the Stewards are still amateur men and women who give their time, experience and wisdom for free. A different panel of Stewards sits at each racecourse. Most other countries employ professional or semi-professional Stewards.

Three-quarters of an hour before the first race there is another, more informal meeting between the Stewards' Secretary, the Stewards, the Chief Veterinary Officer, the Betting Intelligence Officer and possibly the Handicapper. This is to make sure that all favourites and fancied horses that run badly will be dope-tested after their races. It is possible also that the Jockey Club Security will have passed on information. So a pattern for the day's dope-testing is established. Certain horses are routinely dope-tested at every race meeting.

Cause for an enquiry

During a race each Steward concentrates on a different aspect of the contest, often from different positions in the stand, while one will concentrate on the television coverage. The Stewards' Secretaries will accompany them, and the Betting Intelligence Officer will feed through relevant information. The favourite might

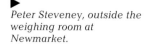
Major Peter Steveney, Stewards' Secretary, in the Stewards' room at Newmarket.

▶
Peter Steveney, outside the weighing room at Newmarket.

Stewards clamber down from their tower at Flemington Park.

be drifting alarmingly, for example, or a previously unfancied horse with no obvious chance on the form be seen to be the subject of substantial last-minute money. The Handicapper, meanwhile, is watching the race from his own special perspective.

Ideally a Stewards' Enquiry is called as the horses flash past the post, though sometimes an announcement may take longer, and any one of the Stewards can demand an Enquiry. If the Steward watching the television sees an incident but does not hear an enquiry called, he will call one himself.

It is part of the Stewards' Secretary's job to bring to the attention of the Stewards (usually four in number) any breach of the Rules in a race if he thinks it has been missed. They have the evidence of camera film of each race taken from different angles. Three stewards will sit on an enquiry, and decision is by a majority vote.

There are 13 Secretaries in all in Great Britain, and Peter Steveney is the most senior or, as he puts it, the "manager of the team". He attends the bigger meetings but finds that he now spends a good deal of his time "managing" at the Jockey Club headquarters, though he makes a point of visiting every racecourse, flat and jumps, once every two years. Altogether he attends around 120 fixtures a year.

Steveney also plays a major part in the training side of the important Stewards' seminars that are organized each spring by the Jockey Club Disciplinary Committee.

There is no doubt that the standard of stewardship at British race meetings has risen over the last few years, and the occasional "bad" decision that is the subject of controversy tends to attract unfavourable press in disproportionate volume compared to the many "good" decisions that pass without any comment whatsoever during each season.

AT THE START

THE STARTER arrives on the course about two hours before the first race, meets up with his assistant and goes through the horses due to run that day. The Assistant Starter (there are five junior starters, who also have responsibility for running the stalls teams) keeps a record of all horses that behave in an abnormal manner at the start – those that need to be blindfolded, or go in to the stalls early or late, or who get upset in the stalls, or who are difficult in any way at all. Together they plan how to load each race.

About half an hour before the first, the Assistant goes down to the start and makes sure the stalls are in the right place and that all the handlers are fit and present. He may go down a bit earlier to conduct stalls tests on any horses that have behaved badly on a previous occasion and who therefore cannot run until receiving a clearance certificate from a licensed Starter.

Before most races the Starter and Assistant will arrive about 10 minutes before the off. If the stalls have been moved from one start to another they are tested. When the horses arrive, the Starter and Assistant check that they are all there and ridden by the right jockeys.

▶ *Former five times champion Willie Carson* (centre), *one of the most experienced and popular jockeys in British racing.*

◀ *At the start.*

They also check the order, and that they are wearing the correct accessories like blinkers and visors. The stalls handlers meanwhile check the girths.

The stalls handlers are perhaps the only professionals on the racecourse who are more familiar to television viewers than to racecourse spectators. Most people have witnessed their sterling work on numerous occasions and often marvelled at the fine blend of patience, firmness, gentleness and courage they use to cajole all but the most obstinate and awkward of animals to enter the stalls.

The Starter calls the draw order – "Carson 1, Eddery 2, Piggott 3" – and sends the odd numbers, with any horses that go in early, round behind the stalls, followed by the even numbers. The loading is supervized by the Assistant. When all is getting near ready, the Starter mounts his rostrum and tells the jockeys to be on their marks – "Two to go, one to go, last one coming in." The Assistant shouts "Gates shut", the foreman of the stalls team and Starter make certain that all the handlers are out of the way. The Starter checks that no horse is unduly upset, or not standing on all four feet, and that all the blinds are removed. He presses the button and ... they're off.

The reluctant starter can cause anxious moments for all before a race, especially a big one, and the stalls handlers have devised various methods of persuading difficult animals to enter the stalls, including placing a blindfold over the horse's head and turning the animal round several times so that, like in a game of blind man's buff, it no longer knows in which direction it is facing. Horses that cause trouble at the start and are reported by the Starter have to then pass a Jockey Club stalls test.

▲
Belmont Park: the start of the State of New York Stakes.

▼
Belmont Park: the gates open.

THE STARTER

IT IS USUALLY the television viewer who witnesses the tense moments, especially before a big race, when all the horses except one are installed. The jockeys, goggles down, are bracing themselves for the vital split-second of the break, and there is the one horse that is acting up and refusing to enter the stalls, and trying everyone's nerves and patience. How long will the Starter give such horses?

Simon Morant is a Jockey Club Starter. "Each case has to be taken on its merits," he replies. "It is very much guid-

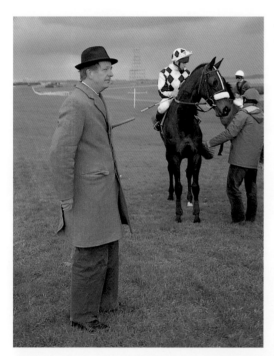

▲
Starter Simon Morant in front of the stalls.

◄
Simon Morant at the start at Newmarket.

▶
Just after the off at Sha Tin.

▼
Out of the stalls at Santa Anita for the Breeders Cup Mile.

small ones, it sometimes happens that you get a big field of good starters and a small field of bad ones.

"On the whole," says Morant, "sprinters are more difficult to deal with than distance horses, being more explosive animals. Big sprints like the Wokingham, the Stewards Cup and the Ayr Gold Cup usually include half a dozen horses which need special treatment. Good horses on the whole behave better at the start than moderate ones. By the end of the season there are about 1,200 horses in the book requiring special treatment of one sort or another, quite a high percentage of those

ed by how the other horses are behaving. If a horse has gone round early, you know it's bad, and if there are no other horses in the stalls you can always spend a bit of time with it because you're not adversely affecting anybody else's chance. But if a horse is causing problems at the end of the loading-up process, and there are many horses in the stalls, some of whom may be growing upset, you obviously have limited patience with it." Sometimes the difficult decision to leave a horse at the start has to be taken, even if that horse has travelled a long way, even from overseas, to line up for a big race.

A Starter attends about 180 fixtures a year (jumping and flat). Though large fields are obviously more tricky than

in training, and there is usually at least one in every race."

Have the stalls ever failed to open? "Yes, but it's rare and happens when the foreman fails to take the catch off one of them and a horse is left behind. Under those circumstances it is a false start and we have to try again. There are not many races left in the British Calendar that are started without stalls – the Chester Cup is one, and the new 2-mile start at Goodwood is a flag start – though sometimes an entire meeting is if the ground is too wet to get the stalls on the course.

"There is no barrier at all in front of the horses on these occasions, and starting them is more difficult than starting jump races where a tape is in use. And the start of a sprint, stalls or no stalls, is terribly important, as everyone is trying to get a flier. Talking of fliers, there is no doubt that it is the top jockeys who are best at the start. If any of them want to get a good start they will."

THE STARTER'S PROCEDURE

The Starter and Assistant arrive at the start.

The stalls are tested.

The horses begin to arrive at the start. Starter and Assistant check that all are present and that the right equipment - blinkers etc - are being worn. Stalls handlers check girths while the Starter calls the draw order. The horses go behind and are loaded into the stalls.

Starter mounts rostrum.

Assistant shouts "Gates shut!"

Starter alerts jockeys, presses the button and "They're off!"

THE CLERK OF THE SCALES

ONE of the pivotal officials on the race-course is the Clerk of the Scales, whose job encompasses much more than merely the weighing out (before the race) and weighing in (after) of the jockeys.

On duty for about 180 long racedays a year (jumping and flat), during which time he clocks up some 20,000 miles travelling, he will arrive some three hours or more before the first race in order to prepare himself for the day's work. He keeps up a work-book containing his necessary information: the day's saddle-cloth numbers, the jockeys due to ride that day, whether they have shown their medical books or not, what allowances any apprentices riding are entitled to (though this is technically still the responsibility of the apprentice and trainer), the weight due to be carried by each horse, the draw, any extras to be carried by each horse over and above the ordinary equipment, such as breast-plates, breast-girths, martingales, blinkers and visors.

The Clerk of the Scales also notes changes of colours (and second and third colours when an owner has more than one horse in a race) and overweights, and makes sure the public is informed. A relatively new duty is to check that every jockey is wearing the now-compulsory back-protector. The credentials and equipment of foreign or occasional jockeys have to be checked. Non-runners (horses that have been withdrawn more than three-quarters of an hour before

▲ ▶
Geoff Hopkins, Clerk of the Scales, weighs out a jockey at Newmarket.

their race) have to be announced to other officials and the public. Special allowances have to be checked against the conditions of a race. Penalties incurred after publication of the weights must be added. Last-minute changes of ownership must be registered. The details and consequences of selling and claiming races also come within the Clerk of the Scales' province.

Suspended riders must be barred from the weighing-room. A horse owned by a person owing money to the racing authorities will not be allowed to run, and the jockey will therefore not be weighed out. The Clerk of the Scales co-

ordinates the radio network that connects all the major officials on the course. And he makes sure that the jockeys' valets sign the forms that entitle them to their very small percentage of each day's stakes.

So the duties of the Clerk of the Scales are rather more onerous than his job description might suggest. Geoffrey Hopkins is the Jockey Club's senior Clerk of the Scales, having been in the job for 20 years, after 30 years with Weatherbys before that.

AT THE SCALES

DURING racing, the Clerk of the Scales' job more accurately fits its title. He checks that each jockey is who he is meant to be and is carrying the right number and wearing the right colours. The jockey sits on the scales with his gear and the weight is checked. Blinkers and visors are examined. All jockeys are now allowed an extra 1lb of weight to allow for the body protector. It is a little-

known fact that each horse in the 1991 Derby therefore carried (9st 1lb), rather than the normal (9st), for the first time in history. Flat pieces of lead, in quarter pounds, half pounds and pounds, are used to make up extra weight and are carried either in pockets in some saddles, or more usually in the weight-cloth. These are adjusted by the valets before the jockeys come to scale.

After each race the Clerk always weighs the first four jockeys. At least once a meeting he calls in all the riders for a spot-check, and all have to weigh when there is a photograph finish and the result is uncertain. All riders are weighed in after apprentice and amateur races. In all cases there is a leeway of minus 1lb and plus 2lb to allow for sweating and inclement weather. Hopkins recalls an occasion when a jockey weighed in at 5lb over, having ridden through a thunderstorm. He only drew the correct weight after taking off his boots and emptying them on the weighing-room floor.

Five minutes after the winning jockey has passed the scales, and providing that no Stewards' Enquiry or objection has been called (in the case of the latter, the Clerk supervises the writing of the form with the jockey), the Clerk issues the "weighed-in" announcement. That effectively means that the result of the race is

▲ *The unmistakeable figure of Lester Piggott in the foreground of a group of jockeys in the weighing room at Newmarket.*

▶ *Willie Carson weighs out for the first in the famous colours of Hamdan Al Maktoum.*

sacrosanct and unalterable except by the Stewards of the Jockey Club in exceptional cases. The Clerk of the Scales can himself object if a jockey fails to weigh in or fails to draw the correct weight. If a jockey is carrying too much weight he is the subject of a report rather than an objection. Fines for jockeys' unexplained misdemeanours may be administered. At busy times the Clerk of the Scales will be weighing out jockeys for the next race at the same time as he is weighing them in for the last.

At the end of each fixture a comprehensive return on the day's racing, a racecard with inter-leaves, along with the Stewards' and Vet's reports and the Judge's and Starter's slips, are prepared for the offical records. The Clerk of the Scales' duties are more far-reaching than his title suggests.

Every so often there are rumours of skullduggery as certain jockeys try to cheat the scales. "A jockey is trying to make a living," Hopkins remarks, "and, yes, there is a running battle between certain jockeys and the Clerks of the Scales. We know them and they know we know them. We make sure it doesn't get out of bounds. The trouble is that there are jockeys who do not get as many rides as they would like and therefore accept rides for which they know they cannot do the weight, despite sweating off as many pounds as possible in the sauna. Jockeys do occasionally attempt to try it on, but on the whole their bluff is called."

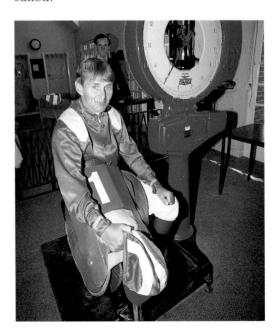

THE RACING COLOURS

NO SET OF RACING COLOURS is the same and all have to be registered with Weatherbys, the Jockey Club's secretariat. Some could hardly be more simple, like the plain apricot favoured by Lord Howard de Walden, while others, like the multi-coloured set first registered by Bud Flanagan of the Crazy Gang, could hardly be more gaudy. Among the more famous currently to be seen on European racecourses are Lord Derby's classic black with white cap, Sheikh Mohammed's maroon, white sleeves and maroon cap with a white star, Hamdan Al Maktoum's royal blue, white epaulets and striped cap, Robert Sangster's emerald green, royal blue sleeves and white cap with emerald green spots, and the Queens' purple, gold braid, scarlet sleeves, and black velvet cap with gold fringe.

▶
Lanfranco Dettori, wearing the colours of Mr. R. L. Duchossois at York.

▼
Michael Roberts, wearing the colours of Sheikh Ahmed Al Maktoum.

◀
Steve Cauthen wearing Sheikh Mohammed's colours at Goodwood.

▶
Ray Cochrane, wearing the colours of Athos Christodoulou

▼
Steve Cauthen, wearing Lord Howard de Walden's colours.

◀
Willie Carson wearing the colours of Sheikh Hamdan Al Maktoum.

▼
Greville Starkey, on Dancing Brave, wearing Khalid Abdullah's colours.

THE ART OF HANDICAPPING

THERE ARE few more fascinating but demanding jobs in the racing world than that of the Handicapper, whether he works for one of the big tipping organizations, or whether he is an official handicapper employed by the Jockey Club. Handicapping is the art of allotting ratings to horses, depending on their performances, which, when translated into racing weights, would in theory so accurately reflect each horse's ability that they would finish in a straight line across the course at the end of a race. The difficult art of handicapping is at the heart of horse racing.

Each of the six official flat racing Handicappers has responsibility for a different section of racing: two-year-olds, 5 and 6 furlongs, 7 to 9 furlongs, 10 to 12

▼ *French trained Miesque lifts the Breeders Cup in 1988.*

furlongs, and longer distances and all-weather racing. Each Handicapper will attend approximately 10 fixtures a month, making a point of travelling to those which include important races in his particular category. There is a Handicapper on duty at most race meetings in the calendar.

Race by race the Handicapper will assess the performances of all the horses at the meeting so that he can not only re-handicap the horses if necessary in his own specialized area, but also pass on to his fellow Handicappers information he considers relevant to theirs. On days when he is not racing he is still constantly handicapping and re-handicapping the horses within his sphere and, through modern computer links, tapping in the revised ratings to Weatherbys, the Jockey Club secretariat.

And so the handicap is in a constant process of updating. The full list of ratings is published every 5 or 6 weeks in a special supplement of the *Racing Calendar* and a list of new ratings is published every week. Ratings range from 0-140, though exceptional horses may be rated higher (in 1986 Dancing Brave was rated 141), and there are always some, thankfully known only to the Handicappers, which are rated below zero. Handicap races are divided as follows: selling handicaps, 0-60; £2,800-£3,500, 0-70; £3,50l-£5,400, 0-80; £4,50l-£6,500, 0-90; £6,50l-£10,000, 0-100; £10,001-£20,000, 0-110; £20,000 +, 0-115.

THE HANDICAPPER'S DAY

On a raceday he will arrive some two hours before the first race in order to discuss the day's racing with the Stewards of the meeting. Throughout the day he will be on hand to guide them in matters of form, and his opinion on whether a horse has run notably above or below its merits may well affect the outcome of a Stewards' Enquiry. He will also be available to discuss the handicapping of horses with owners and trainers and other interested parties. This is particularly important

in the spring when horses may or may not have trained on from the previous season, and their form may have to be radically reassessed. Trainers and owners frequently complain that the Handicapper has overrated their animals, and that they are therefore set to carry too much weight in forthcoming races. In the upper echelons of the sport, when an animal is running in Group rather than handicap class, it is even possible to hear them complain that their animal has been underrated.

THE SENIOR HANDICAPPER

GEOFFREY GIBBS is the Jockey Club's Senior Handicapper and, though he is too modest a man to admit it, he probably knows as much about the form and handicapping of racehorses as anyone on the planet. He is completely frank about his gentle art: "The basic truth is that you cannot be right in handicapping. All you can do is assess the information you have in front of you and what you have seen with your own eyes. But there is no question of being right. Indeed, every time a race is run you're proved wrong."

Certainly many trainers, and often those that are quick to complain about injustices, do not understand the ins and outs of handicapping like he does, and even those that do seldom have the nec-

◀ *Geoffrey Gibbs, Senior Handicapper to the Jockey Club.*

essary time to give to the subject. On the other hand, a trainer will know a great deal about his own charges and will be able to give the handicapper a lot of information, some useful, some less so, about them. On the whole, the Handicappers are ready and willing to help trainers with a genuine grievance, though they are unlikely to be very happy if they then see the animal in question backed from 10 to 5/1 and winning by 4 lengths doing handsprings.

Gibbs readily admits that it is impossible to satisfy everybody.

"If you have 12 runners in a handicap, only one person will be satisfied at the finish and that will be the winner."

A particular difficulty of handicapping is whether, when a horse keeps winning, to reassess the horses that he has previously run against or whether to take the view that the horse in question is the improving horse and that the others should be left. Certain trainers have had particular success in handicaps by appearing to keep their horses improving faster than the Handicapper can get to grips with them. They then claim that they suffer from that success, as the Handicappers are hesitant to take a chance with their horses.

"What Cumani was doing", says Gibbs, "was using the handicap system to take a potential Group horse through

ADMIRAL ROUS AND THE BEAUTIFUL THEORY

One of the greatest figures in the history of the turf was Admiral Henry John Rous (1795-1877), who took the post of public Handicapper in 1855 at the age of 60. Current Senior Handicapper Geoffrey Gibbs believes that the following passage, taken from Rous' On the Laws and Practice of Horse-racing *(1850), best sums up the problems that still beset the handicappers each day:*

Racing is a game ruled by the weights and scales; and the scientific branch of racing is to be enabled to form a correct judgement of the influence every pound of extra weight will make between horses of the same calibre – always presuming that the horses are fit to run, and are meant to win. Matches and handicaps are experimental trials of the particular effect of certain weights on the presumed speed or stoutness of any two or more horses in a given distance; but handicapping on a large scale, with the idea that you can bring one hundred horses within the length of a room at the end of two miles, is a beautiful theory, never to be reduced to practice. Every great handicap offers a premium to fraud; mares seldom run in their best form before the month of August; and geldings are considered to be best in the spring.

Taking therefore into consideration the differences of opinion respecting individual condition, the effect of weight on the comparative qualifications of the horses engaged, the possible indisposition of some of them, the unequal merits of the jockeys, and the uncertain state of the ground, it is not to be wondered that races resolve themselves into problems difficult of solution; and this constitutes the greatest interest in racing, or what is called "the glorious uncertainty of the turf."

its races, giving it invaluable experience without having to ask it too serious a question. This is a perfectly legitimate method. As long as a horse has either won a race or run three times, it can be entered in handicaps. It might win three races before we catch up with it, though with the new entry system it is more difficult than it was, as you now race off the same mark for a maximum of twelve days instead of a possible five weeks. Under the old system, after all, Chaplin's Club managed to win seven races before the Handicapper got his measure."

Gibbs seldom looks at commercial handicapping publications, though he makes the point that just because he works for the Jockey Club it does not mean he is any better than them. There is no doubt that his task is harder than theirs, however, for while they are picking out one horse in a handicap that might win, he is trying to give an opportunity to win to all the runners. In a handicap for three-year-olds and up there is a weight range of 35lb. There may be 30 entries for the race, and if 18 of them stand their ground when the weights are published, the Handicapper has done the first part of his job, especially if the acceptors are spread across the weight range.

If on the day of the race the betting is fairly open, going perhaps 4/1 the field, then the Handicapper can justifiably feel fairly satisfied. Even so, he will probably by then be able to look at his own handicap and pick out two or three runners that are actually likely to win, taking in considerations such as the ground, the draw, their fitness, their liking for the course and so on. The fact that one of the other runners then goes and spreadeagles his field by a comfortable 3½ lengths is a circumstance beyond his control. Close finishes are anyway determined to a large extent by the distance of the race. Sprints are far more likely to make the judge call for a photograph than a 2-mile event.

"The weight is an important ingredient," says Gibbs, "but there are probably 15 other factors that are just as significant. If 9 of the 16 factors that affect a horse are against him, it doesn't matter at all what weight he's got. He's not going to win."

One of these important factors, in Gibbs's opinion, is the jockey.

► *Lanfranco Dettori after a fall.*

"It is not chance that the top jockeys keep getting the best rides. At the moment Frankie Dettori is everybody's idea of a future champion jockey. He has had the benefit of being attached to Luca Cumani's stable and has the intelligence and ability to have made the best of that situation. But there is no doubt that when he or any of the top jockeys get on to a horse, the very fact that they are riding winners, are confident, and have a positive attitude as to what they're going to do in a race, contributes to the horse's performance. But a jockey who has had a bad run makes mistakes. Instead of going to the front when he should, he decides

▼ *Geoffrey Gibbs (right), Senior Handicapper, with trainer Luca Cumani, who has proved himself a master of placing his horses to win good handicaps.*

to wait a bit longer, or he comes too soon, or he finds himself boxed in on the rails. He loses the confidence required for successful race-riding."

One of the aspects of racing on which Geoffrey Gibbs is particularly fascinating is its growing internationalism. To the question about how difficult is it to compare racing from country to country and from continent to continent, he replies with a disarming "It's not." For nearly a decade he has been monitoring all the American Graded Stakes, similar to British Group races. He goes to the USA two or three times a year and has built up excellent working relations with "the race secretaries" – American handicappers. Together they plan by 1995 to publish jointly at the end of each year a definitive Northern Hemisphere Classification.

"Last year there were three horses which appeared both in the American Blood Horse Free Handicap and in our own Free Handicap and they were relatively all the same 4lb apart in each. And when it comes to the older horses – and the Breeders Cup Series has borne this out – handicappers on both sides of the Atlantic can independently produce figures that are seldom more than 2lb or 3lb apart. That is remarkable. And it is remarkable too that horses from Europe are able to go across to America and run within 1lb of their European form,

▲
Lashkari wins the Breeders Cup in 1984.

▼
Smile wins the sprint race for the Breeders Cup in 1986.

despite the travelling, the very different climate and the dirt surface they encounter."

There is no doubt that the Handicapper's life is a stressful one, particularly since the five-day entry system has meant that they now have five deadlines a week rather than one. On the other hand, they now have the satisfaction of seeing horses running off their right marks, and the correction of work is thus easier. But the increasing internationalism of racing and the ever-growing horse population has seen the Handicapper's workload get heavier over the years, and it is probable that it will become

◀▶
*Racecourse commentators
Bruce Friend-James* (right)
and Robin Gray (left).

THE RACECOURSE COMMENTATOR

ROBIN GRAY, racing correspondent for the *News of the World*, and Bruce Friend-James are racecourse commentators. Because of Newmarket's layout, both are needed in races of 1 mile or more, when one takes up position down the course to let the public know what is happening while the runners are out of sight or mere specks in the distance. At other courses more than one commentator is employed only on the big occasions, or when there are more than 115 horses declared to race in one day.

The commentators' job is to describe the action as informatively, accurately and entertainingly as possible. "Entertainingly" is a relatively new part of the job description. It was not long ago that listening to a racecourse commentary was about as entertaining as watching paint dry. The original brief, when racecourse commentating began some 35 years ago, was to be totally factual, never get excited, and never mention an incident. Things are livelier these days. The modern trend is to inject a bit of flavour and excitement into the development of a horserace. But accuracy is still paramount, and the racecourse commentator cannot let himself get carried away like some of his colleagues on the TV and radio. And nowadays the commentator keeps going as the horses pass the line and tries to give the order if possible, without pre-empting the judge in close finishes.

TV AND RADIO COMMENTATORS

Some of the most familiar voices and faces in racing belong to the TV and radio racing journalists. Still by far the most famous of the commentators is the veteran Peter O'Sullevan, whose stylish, controlled and exact rise to the climax has been much imitated but seldom equalled. On BBC radio Peter Bromley has painted an exciting and vivid word-picture of many a big race

While BBC TV can still do justice to the big occasion like Royal Ascot, it refuses to offer a total commitment to the sport. Meanwhile Channel 4 Racing, under the leadership of Brough Scott, has become the most professional outfit on television. Its superb coverage all but transports the viewer to the racetrack and manages to convey much of the atmosphere and excitement of a day at the races. The paddock commentaries of John Oaksey and John Francome are certainly the most entertaining, if not the most informative, in the sport.

▶
Brough Scott conducting an interview.

Robin Gray marks up his racecard with the relevant colours and learns them between races. Another commentator might do this overnight. Learning the colours presents much less of a problem than bad angles or bad light. However, good camera coverage of all races is a great boon to the racecourse commentator, who can now make use of the monitors, although they often find themselves doing so in bright sunlight.

Every commentator has the spectre of some terrible mental aberration hanging over him. In Gray's case the nightmare once became reality in the Cesarewitch at Newmarket some years ago. Another commentator, John Hickman, handed over to him 5 furlongs out and Gray called a certain horse all the way to the line. It was only when it flashed past the winning post in the lead that he realized he had been calling the wrong horse. "It

took a long time for my confidence to recover after that."

Bruce Friend-James is quick to put this into perspective. "If you're patient, sooner or later you will find that every commentator makes a mistake. We're only human after all. We've all made the same mistake on lesser occasions. Robin was particularly unlucky because it happened to be a very important race." It is Robin Gray who often calls the Derby, and on an occasion of such great importance he has an assistant commentator speaking into one ear, pointing out any errors he may have made or anything he may have missed.

Certainly the commentator's lot is more difficult in Britain than anywhere else in the world. In Australia there is no straight course longer than 7 furlongs, while in America $1\frac{1}{2}$ miles is as big as a track ever gets.

▼
Racecourse commentators Bruce Friend-James and Robin Gray make last minute checks on the racecourse before a cold day's racing at Newmarket's Craven Meeting.

THE JOCKEYS

The life of the top jockey is perhaps busier and tougher than that of any other professional sportsman. Up with the lark, he is riding work on the gallops long before most people are awake, sometimes having travelled long distances to do so. He may ride out several lots in a morning before setting off to the races by car or plane. During the summer months he may ride at two meetings a day, at afternoon and evening meetings, perhaps partnering a dozen different horses, before returning late at night from some far distant fixture.

And then there are all the calls to make, the trainers and owners to talk to, the form to be studied, the rides to be booked. In recent years most of the top riders have begun to use agents to do this part of their work for them, as they

Steve Cauthen and Reference Point in the most hallowed unsaddling enclosure in the world, after winning the 1987 Epsom Derby with a thrilling pillar to post ride.

Michael Roberts and Mtoto land the King George VI and Queen Elizabeth Diamond Stakes, the greatest all-age race in the British calendar.

Steve Cauthen and Old Vic after winning Le Prix du Jockey Club, the French Derby.

Pat Valenzuela, star of the American circuit.

No star is rising faster than that of Lanfranco Dettori, Luca Cumani's brilliant young jockey.

simply have not had the time to do it for themselves. A top jockey will take some 800 to 900 mounts a season in Britain alone. At weekends, and for big races during the week, he will often find himself jetting off to France, Ireland, Germany, Italy, and nowadays to Japan, the USA and all points of the compass.

While the rewards are great, the pressures are intense. One bad ride and a jockey can fall from grace with the notoriously fickle racing world, and there is nothing quite so unfashionable as an unfashionable jockey. Meanwhile, life at the top is an exhausting process, and towards the end of the long, grinding season the leading riders begin to show their fatigue, often exacerbated by frequent gruelling sessions in the sauna desperately trying to shed weight, and the tireder you are the more irksome the shedding of weight becomes.

Michael Roberts is comparatively lucky in that respect as, in his mid-thirties, he is able to ride at 7st 13lb without too much effort. From his childhood days it had always been a dream of his to come to ride in Britain.

"British racing is the best in the world," he states unequivocally. "You have the best horses and the best bloodlines here, and since I was a kid I've always been an admirer of the likes of Lester Piggott, Geoff Lewis and Joe Mercer. They all used to come out to South Africa for the Internationals when I began racing as an apprentice in 1968."

Roberts had a first taste of British racing in 1978, enjoyed himself and always wanted to return one day. When he had achieved everything there was to achieve in his home country, he decided to give it a try. One of the great differences between the two countries is the enormous variety of tracks in Britain compared to their general sameness in South Africa.

"In South Africa they are mainly modern, properly laid-out tracks, without even undulations, whereas here many are just bits of virgin land where someone's put rails up and called it a racecourse. And back home we don't have all these mile and 6 and 2-mile races. We go more for speed. We have our Gold Cup races, but our average distance would be about 9 furlongs."

MICHAEL ROBERTS

Michael Roberts, the former 11-times champion jockey of South Africa, has in recent years established himself as one of the most sought-after jockeys currently riding in Britain. He first rode his way into the headlines with his exploits on Mtoto, and since 1988 he has joined the elite handful of jockeys capable of riding 100 and more winners in a season. Always in great demand, his career is still in the ascendance, and he is now in a position to mount a challenge for the British championship. He is retained by trainer Alec Stewart, Clive Brittain having second claim.

▼
The Queen presents Michael Roberts with his memento after his victory on Mtoto at Ascot in the King George and Queen Elizabeth Diamond Stakes.

▲
Michael Roberts, currently one of the most sought-after riders on the European circuit.

◄
The return of the Longfellow. In 1990 Lester Piggott astounded the racing world by announcing his comeback. Here he is seen at Newmarket in 1991 wearing the colours of his old friend Charles St. George and that familiar quizzical expression.

►
Walter Swinburn on Shaadi. Walter shot to fame with his Derby victory on Shergar and has remained in the forefront ever since.

RIDING STYLES

THE BRITISH weighing-rooms have become well-used to foreign riders. Most have had to adapt their styles to fit in with the British style of racing, however, and South African jockey Michael Roberts is no exception.

"The horses are very well schooled in Britain and much more laid-back to ride," he comments. "At home they see the gates and they want to run, but here you have to make them go. Riding styles change from country to country. In the States it's speed all the way. They sit in behind their horses' ears, practically lying flat on their backs. Personally I prefer the English way.

"Every jockey has his different, set way of riding. Cauthen is a front-riding jockey. Coming from America he has learnt to do everything by the clock. But of course it all depends upon the horse you are riding and what suits it best. If they're not going any great pace it's probably best to be out in front and out of trouble, letting the horse bowl along and enjoy itself. A great deal of judgement has to go into riding from behind, and traffic problems are the main worry.

"There are more tactics involved in riding from behind. When you're in front you obviously try to conserve some of the horse's energy for the finishing effort, but if you're on the best horse anyway it doesn't matter too much, because they won't be able to reach you."

▲
A race develops at Sandown Park, the highly popular course on the outskirts of London.

Another difference between racing in Britain and elsewhere that Roberts has had to confront lies in the training process. In other countries it is customary to ride quite a lot of work on the same track that you will be racing on later in the day, and you might ride 20 horses in a

morning. In Britain it might take an hour to ride one particular horse at work, and it is physically impossible to ride more than three or four in a morning.

There are also great differences between the detailed methods of training in Britain and elsewhere. Roberts was very surprised when he first encountered the English method.

"The English lads have a real relationship with their animals. They really love

▶ *Trainer Luca Cumani in the Longchamp paddock stands with two of the Aga Khan's jockeys before the 1988 Prix de L'Arc de Triomphe.*

▼ *The names of amateur women jockeys are chalked up alongside those of the hardened professionals for a rare mixed race.*

4.40	DICKINS INVITATION STAKES	
1	G.STARKEY	2
2	Maxine.JUSTER	10
3	T.IVES	3
4	Brooke.SANDERS	8
5	Jennie.GOULDING	5
6	Joanna.WINTER	6
7	W.R.SWINBURN	1
8	B.THOMSON	4
9	S.CAUTHEN	7
10	Carolyn.EDDERY	9
	10.RUNNERS	

their horses and the job they're doing. Back home it's just a routine affair. Take the horse out, work it, take it back to the yard and groom it, and that's the end of that. The South African horses probably look better than the horses do here, because of the sun and the weather, and also because they're a more robust type of horse. But considering the climate they really look wonderful over here, surprisingly so."

▶ *Lady jockeys. Despite the success of such as Alex Greaves and Kim Tinkler, no female jockey in Britain has yet made it to the highest level, and various prejudices are still held about their strength and capability. But it is just a question of time.*

He cast his expert eye over a field of maidens walking round the Newmarket parade ring. "Look how nice and quiet and relaxed those horses are. At home, with less good staff, they are always on their toes and tensed up and wanting to get on with the business."

Michael Roberts is a natural jockey. He has that certain, indefinable rapport with horses which makes them want to run for him. He has succeeded where other jockeys before him have failed in making the tricky transition from one continent to another, from one style to another. Perhaps Roberts was helped by the fact that from his childhood his admiration for English racing led him to base his style on some of his English heroes, riding fairly short but with a long rein. He has always believed in letting the horse do the work for him, giving him as much rein as possible and getting him to relax.

"I think in terms of style I was halfway there when I came over. All I had to do was to give my style a bit more drive. I think English trainers like to see drive rather than the whip going bang, bang, bang, which happens a lot at home. In South Africa if you don't use the whip the Stewards want to know what's wrong with you. That's one aspect that I've worked on and improved in my riding. But to start changing styles at my age is hard, and it's no use trying to copy other jockeys because nine out of ten times their style won't suit you. Everyone to their own style. Mine's been successful for me, so why change? There are always people ready to criticize some little aspect of your riding."

THE APPRENTICE JOCKEYS

Apprentice jockeys line up at Sandown. A good apprentice can be worth his weight in gold, but many have problems graduating to become fully-fledged jockeys when they have lost their allowances.

In the last forty years, the apprentice championship has been won by some names that were soon to become illustrious: Lester Piggott, Joe Mercer, Edward Hide, Greville Starkey, Bruce Raymond, Sandy Barclay, Pat Eddery and Lanfranco Dettori

among them. But other top apprentices have failed to make the transition to jockey and have gradually faded from view. Certain trainers have made a habit of producing good apprentices, Reg Hollinshead, and the late Frenchie Nicholson among others. An effective apprentice is soon in great demand among the other stables, and many is the time when the result of an important handicap has been decided by a boy who is really worth his allowance.

THE JOCKEY'S VALET

WHEN IT comes to the hardest-working man on the racecourse there is no competition. He is the jockey's valet. He is responsible for looking after and cleaning

Michael Hales, jockeys' valet, one of the hardest-working men on the turf.

Jockeys' silks.

the tack, boots, britches and saddles of his jockeys – everything they wear, in fact, except the colours (the responsibility of the stable). It is he who lugs the jockeys' equipment from course to course, producing it spotless and gleaming on every occasion, piles it mud-spattered and battered into the back of his car every night, and is back in the weighing-room next morning with it all looking like new again.

There are about fifteen jockey's valets in all. Some have been known to fall by the wayside. It seems they just couldn't stand the pace.

Not so jockey's valet extraordinary, Michael (Mick) Hales. Just listen to his demanding routine.

"Unless I stay away for a big meeting, I am always up by 7 o'clock. I bring all the tack to the racecourse, clean it up, sort it out and lay it out so that it's ready for the jockeys just to walk in, put it on and go out and ride. For each race I change the colours for them and hang them up on the wall. Then I sort out the colour bags with the head lads.

"While the jockeys rush in and out from race to race I'm getting the saddles and the weights right for their next ride. There are about 60 jockeys in all that I do for, and probably about a dozen a day on average. Ten or twelve, in fact, is quite enough. My estate car is full to the roof with gear every time I set out to or come back from a meeting. I am always the first into and the last out of the weighing-room, and if I get away an hour and a half after the last I think myself lucky."

Mick says that the essential character of the job has changed a good deal over the years.

"In the old days the valet was a proper valet, like a gentleman's gentleman," (Mick says this without a trace of scorn, indeed with a hint of nostalgia), "but now

▼
All spick and span, jockeys head towards the paddock for the third.

it's just a matter of getting there, getting the job done as quick as you can, and getting on to the next meeting. Much of the fun and mutual respect has gone out of the world.

"It's all big business now," says Mick.

"In days gone by it was all done for the people that were in racing. The mugs were the ones who came to the races without knowing anything about it. But now with all the media and television coverage, a dustman knows as much about it as I do."

But the weighing-room banter and camaraderie still remain, at least when the racing isn't too serious, and there is still time for a joke or two. When there is a lot of money at stake the jockeys tend to get rather more tensed up.

"That's when they get upset very easily and you have to watch it, though afterwards it's all forgotten." And no doubt that was always the case.

Mick's family have been jockeys' valets for three generations. His grandfather looked after legendary names like Steve Donaghue and Brownie Carslake, and none more legendary than the great Fred Archer himself.

Mick's grandfather also "did" Lester Piggott, then a boy of 12, for his first ever ride back in 1948. How remarkable that one man linked the two greatest legends of the turf, one who went to an early grave in the same year that Gottlieb Daimler invented the world's first motor-bike, the other still battling for the top prizes as the computer age hurtles towards the 21st century. Mick's father soon took over doing Piggott, then Mick himself did the great man for 17 years.

For 7 months of the year, the flat-racing season, he works 6 days a week, and he has hardly ever missed a fixture since he started. That it is extremely hard work goes without saying, and now in the winter months, when previously he would be taking a well-earned rest and going to a few jump meetings for fun, there is the all-weather racing to be dealt with.

▶
A mud spattered Billy Newnes returns on Transcript, demonstrating that some days are even worse than usual for the valet.

THE JOCKEY'S EQUIPMENT

The kind of equipment a jockey uses in a race may vary between trainers, and may depend on the stature and idiosyncrasies of the horse. Good racing saddles are of the utmost importance but they are expensive. Jockeys may need three saddles on average in a day's racing.

Under the saddle there are three layers – the number-cloth, the weight-cloth and a sheet of foam rubber. The saddle is held firmly in position by the girth, which is buckled under a flap on each side. As a protection against bruising, and sometimes bone-breaking falls, the jockey wears a back protector, or corset, under the riding silk.

The cap is a protective helmet which the Clerk of the Scales does not include in the weighing in and out. As a result, jockeys are not tempted to save a little weight by wearing a light cap that might endanger their lives in a fall.

The martingale, made up of two metal rings joined by a leather strap, prevents the reins from rising over the head of the horse.

A weight-cloth has pockets into which strips of lead are placed when the weight of the jockey and equipment needs to be increased to a level required by the race.

A back-protector, worn under the silk, provides a measure of added safety in the event of a fall.

Saddles are usually made of leather and may be between 1lb and 9lb.

The number-cloth is thin and light and serves to indicate the number of the horse in a race.

BLINKERS AND HOODS

A horse may wear blinkers to help concentration during a race – these restrict vision and force the horse to look straight ahead. And if the horse is easily distracted by noise, a hood – with holes for the eyes – can be used to cover the ears.

A hood covering the ears prevents the horse being distracted by noise.

Blinkers reduce the horse's vision from 180° to about 30°.

A slit in each blinker allows the horse to see his rivals.

◀
A certain Parisian elegance flavours the paddock at Longchamp.

▼
Royal Ascot. The Sangsters flank black-hatted trainer Barry Hills.

THE PADDOCK

THE ATMOSPHERE around the paddock before a big race is electric. Long before the first horse enters the parade ring the public are lined up several rows deep on all sides. Then come the equine stars, led

▼
Horses and jockeys about to leave the paddock at Sandown Park, perhaps the most comfortable and best laid-out of British courses.

by their devoted lads, glistening and gleaming and fit to run for their lives.

Spotting the connections is a game played by large sections of the public. Apart from providing innocent amusement, it can furnish genuinely useful information that cannot be gleaned elsewhere. If Hamdam Al-Maktoum is seen in the paddock before a lowly maiden race at a small track, for example, it is a safe bet that great things are expected from his representative.

Then there is always the dilemma encountered by the fashionable trainer with two or more runners in the same race. Which of them will he go to when the time comes to give the jockey the leg-up, and which will have to make do with the assistant or the lad? There are possibly profitable pointers to be interpreted here by the eagle-eyed paddock punter, who lives in the hope that the trainer will be the making a great fuss of the same horse at the other end of a successful race.

THE PARADE

Quest for Fame in the Derby Parade.

Jockey Club rules state that there must be a parade before all Group One races. Many trainers are critical of the parade, claiming that it does nothing but harm to the more nervous and highly-strung sort of animal. On the other hand, the parade enables all sections of the racecourse, including the Silver Ring, to see all the horses at close quarters. Matters are taken to an extreme before the Derby when the horses are required not only to parade, but then to cross the downs through the melee of people, funfairs, buses, noise and bustle, in order to reach the start. Again, many people are critical of this arrangement, but others claim that this is all part of the reason why the Derby is still the greatest test of a Thoroughbred in the world. If he can get through the preliminaries and still perform well, they argue, then he not only has the necessary ability, but also the temperament to go with it.

In the United States there is more clamour, glamour and showbiz attached to horseracing in general, making its English cousin seem quite staid and frumpy. There the horses are flanked by outriders during the parade, while the commentator would never be content to limit himself to the factual remarks of his English counterpart. The jockeys ride in a crouching, streamlined style, pointing their sticks in the air, and the pace is usually flat out from pillar to post. The winner seldom arrives back to the polite handclapping of a British crowd but to a tumultuous roar of approval.

▲▲
Wise after the event: Willie Carson explains exactly what went right to trainer Dick Hern (wheelchair), owner Mana Al-Maktoum and racing manager Angus Gold.

▲
The Maktoum family, owners of the world's best bloodstock, in the winners' enclosure at Royal Ascot.

THE POST MORTEM

AFTER a 12-runner race, the winning team are "over the moon" and one or two other stables may have been pleased by their horses running better than expected. Everybody else indulges in post mortems.

These take place at a variety of venues: as the jockey and horse come in off the track, the trainer jogging along anxiously by their side; as the jockey scurries back towards the weighing-room carrying his saddle and weight-cloth but still keeping two steps ahead of the disappointed owner; as the horse is being hosed down in the racecourse stables by lads who have just been parted from their hard-earned pay; as trainer and wife drive grim-faced up the motorway to complete the round trip from stable to racecourse and back again.

The most public post mortems take place in the unsaddling enclosure, where the connections of well-backed favourites stare at horse and jockey accusingly, scratch their heads and ponder on the circumstances that led to them finishing a poor third. The jockey, anxious to regain the sanctuary of the weighing-room but conscious of the need to offer palliatives to bemused and long-suffering owners, mutters well-worn phrases like "He just wasn't the same horse as last time," or "He'd be better over a trip," or even "I think he must have swallowed his tongue going into Swinley Bottom."

Then they rush away to the scales, the changing-room and the next ride, leaving the trainer to puzzle over what really went wrong.

Some trainers are extraordinarily adept at finding excuses for their horses' dismal performances and can perform thrilling feats of verbal tightrope walking, blaming almost everyone and everything that has ever come into contact with the animal without casting the least aspersion on themselves. On rare occasions they find themselves in front of the Stewards trying to explain why their horse, backed down to favourite from 8/1, has suddenly run far better than expected. Here their verbal dexterity is particularly useful.

On the whole, though, the lesser lights of the training profession spend most of their time making excuses for bad, rather than good, performances. Perhaps they should follow the example of Henry Cecil who, when asked to explain why his horses almost always, even in defeat,

◄
After his sensational comeback victory in the Breeders Cup, Lester Piggott watches the replay.

THE PRESS CONFERENCE

David Elsworth talks to the press at Kempton Park.

Impromptu press conferences are held by the successful, and occasionally the unsuccessful, trainer in the winners' enclosure. Almost engulfed by gentlemen from the press, he agrees that the performance just witnessed was indeed a particularly fine one, implies that this was a training feat nothing short of the miraculous, especially considering the problems with the horse's off fore, reminds those with short memories that the colt was bought at a bargain price on his particular recommendation and despite doubts in certain quarters, and then hints that there are several more at home who could be as good or better, though he won't be drawn on their names.

At this point Brough Scott's runner appears and begs a television interview. The trainer readily agrees, as long as he is not questioned on the "Flashy Boy affair", over which the Disciplinary Committee of the Jockey Club is still puzzling. In front of the camera the trainer repeats all he has said to the other journalists but rather more boisterously. He remembers just in time to thank his staff, "who deserve all the credit for this win," though this is somehow less convincing than some parts of his patter, and finishes off by reminding the viewers that though his services are in great demand he happens by chance to have a few empty boxes at home that could do with being filled.

turn in decent performances, looked at his interrogator as though he might not be all there. "Well, I only run them when they're fit," he replied.

The worst sort of post mortems are those indulged in by a hostile crowd, particularly a French crowd. The unfortunate trainer or jockey, held by the mob, usually unfairly, to have failed in his duties, is jeered and jostled and whistled at and has occasionally to be escorted from the course for his own safety.

THE PRESS ROOM

ONE OF the more comfortable places from which to watch a day's racing is the Press Room. Usually well sited, it has the additional advantage of providing free refreshments to the racing journalists who follow round the racing circus and who are the lucky possessors of a coveted silver badge, giving access to any course in the country. Photographers, too, make use of the free beer and sandwiches before embarking on their day's business, which involves a good deal of running about from paddock to track to unsaddling enclosure and back to paddock again.

The pressmen come in all shapes and sizes. There are the well-paid and elegantly-dressed racing correspondents of the national papers. These lucky souls are able to make a good living by scribbling a few words each day about the sport they love. Many of them eschew

the Press Room for much of the time, preferring to lounge around the weighing-room, unsaddling enclosure and paddock, where they can concentrate on the fine art of seeing and being seen. After an impressive performance they collect in a huddle around the winning trainer hoping for quotable remarks and useful information.

There are the professional race-readers, employed by one of the big form-book operations or the racing newspapers. These highly skilled men and women can watch a race, even a 30-runner sprint, and not only tell you the

▶
American trainer, Shug McGaughey.

▶
Shug McGaughey faces the press.

▲ *Alex Greaves returns on Amenable after winning the Lincoln Handicap, the biggest victory yet in Britain by a woman jockey.*

▼ *Alex Greaves holds court after her famous win.*

oxtondod finishing order and how each horse performed, but very often, and with some accuracy, how each horse will perform next time too.

On Saturdays the number in the Press Room is swelled by assistants from the newspaper racing desks who are stuck in their offices all week and take advantage of free passes at weekends to celebrate their temporary freedom. At the end of each day's sport, articles are dashed off, phone calls made to the copytakers who wait patiently back at the newspapers' sports desks, and everyone prepares for the journey home again.

▲ *A group of racing journalists prepare to take notes at Newmarket.*

The atmosphere in the Press Room, emanating especially from the older members of the profession, is a world-weary, cynical one of "we've seen it all before". Only the relatively few of the corps, who actually love horses, rather than just the racing of horses, are not afflicted by this scepticism. Various racecourse rumours are bandied about. Most turn out to be false, but occasionally one turns into a decent story. And occasionally a really sensational performance sets the place alight and brings words of praise to the lips of even the most travelled and hardened reporter.

THE ART OF THE TIC-TAC MAN

On British racecourses, the bookies add an element of excitement and colour – a raffish air of intrigue, exclusiveness and 'being in the know' that is lacking in many other countries (apart, of course, from a one or two ex-British colonial outposts, such as South Africa).

In Tattersalls Enclosure, the tic-tac men relay shifts in the odds to their colleagues in a sign language that is a mystery to the average racegoer yet remains

◄

Many tic-tac men wear white gloves to be more easily distinguished by their colleagues.

▲ *The tic-tac man makes the signal for odds of even money.*

▲ *Touching his shoulder with the fingers of one hand means horse number five or odds of five to one.*

▲ *Moving his hand and arm, from one shoulder across his body to the crook of the opposite arm, the tic-tac man signals odds of eleven to two.*

arguably more accurate and speedy than the use of any number of walkie-talkies.

Individual idiosyncrasies make it hard to be categorical, but below is a selection of signals used by one tic-tac man.

With his fingers touching his head , he indicates odds of nine to four.

He completes the signal for odds of eleven to eight.

When his fingers touch his chin, it means horse number three or odds of three to one.

Touching the top of his head with his hand means horse number one.

With one hand on his head, the other moving from side to side, the tic-tac man indicates horse number nine or odds of nine to one.

With his hand under his chin, followed by the fingertips of both hands touching, the tic-tac man signals odds of one hundred to thirty.

TRANSCRIPT'S THIRD OUTING

A LONG, cold winter passed between Transcript's last run in 1990 and her first of 1991, a winter that included one of the severest freeze-ups for some years, and the talk in racing centred upon how badly held up in their work and backward most strings would be. Transcript had come into fast work towards the end of April and had continued to please her trainer. Brittain's policy is not to overtax his horses on the gallops, and Transcript was already pretty fit by then.

When it came to choosing a race, there were various alternatives. Eventually Clive narrowed it down to a good maiden at Sandown, in which there were likely to be a large number of runners, or, far more ambitiously, the Marley Roof Oaks Trial Stakes at Lingfield, a Listed race

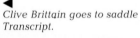
Transcript in the parade ring at Lingfield.

◄
Clive Brittain goes to saddle Transcript.

worth £14,230 to the winner, in which Transcript would be thrown into potential Classic company. Clive plumped for the Oaks Trial, part of his reasoning being that the race might well cut up into only four or five runners, and if Transcript then ran into a place she would herself some much sought after "black type", so called after the type in which placed horses in Pattern races are presented in the sales catalogues (*see p24*). Black type would much enhance

Transcript's value and prospects as a brood mare. If she ran really well, the plan was to send her for the Group One Oaks d'Italia at San Siro. But, sadly, it was not to be.

On a warm but overcast Saturday at Lingfield, Transcript started as the 33/l outsider of seven for the Oaks Trial Stakes over 1m 3 furlongs 106 yards. She was drawn 1, not that the draw made much difference, and the going was on the fast side of good. Neither the ground nor the track – often compared to Epsom, Lingfield puts emphasis on agility and balance rather than galloping and stamina – were thought to be in her favour.

Nevertheless she looked magnificent in the paddock, immaculately turned out as to be expected from Brittain's yard, and a size larger than some of her rivals: Paul Cole's Ausherra, winner of a Kempton maiden on her very first outing as a two-year-old and subsequently second to the useful Jaffa Line in the Group Three Prestige Stakes at Goodwood; the Michael Stoute-trained Campestral, winner of her only race, a decent two-year-old maiden at Newmarket; Gavin Wragg's Gai Bulga, winner of her first race, a three-year-old maiden at Pontefract and subsequently second in a better race at Newmarket; the maiden Killick, the mount of Pat Eddery; Henry Cecil's Owler, the very easy winner of

Transcript circles round before the start.

Michael Hills takes her to post.

her only race, a Beverley maiden, some three weeks previously; and Subtle Change from Guy Harwood's stable, veteran of five races as a two-year-old including victory in a small maiden at Beverley. Apart from Transcript, only Campestral and Subtle Change had not had the benefit of a previous outing as a three-year-old. On the form, and in the minds of the bookies, Transcript was outclassed. And so it proved.

In the paddock before the race, Clive Brittain had told jockey Michael Hills, now the filly's third pilot in as many races, that she was a bit on the lazy side and probably wouldn't like the ground, but to keep her as handy as possible and to make the running if nobody else wanted to, as her stamina did not seem in doubt. Clive thought she would get 1½ miles on good ground, and that 1¼ miles with the

good cut in the ground that she preferred would be perfect. Ausherra duly won the contest, with Gai Bulga second and Subtle Change third. From the public's point of view, joint-favourite Owler was the disappointment of the race, finishing back in sixth place, 6 lengths in front of Transcript, who finished plum last, over 20 lengths behind the winner. Always in the rear, she had failed to go the pace when they quickened up.

In racing it is amazing just how quickly one does come to terms with disappointments. They are far more common than surprise successes, and if coming to terms with them wasn't relatively easy, the tops of racecourse stands would be knee deep in people queuing up to jump off. In the case of Transcript, time for her to win a race before this book went to press was now running out. We had waited interminably for her to run as a two-year-old, and now here she was running last – on television too, to rub salt in the wound – in her first run as a three-year-old. Michael Hills reported afterwards that she certainly wasn't useless. Clive Brittain had seemed confident that she would come on for the race and that a nice maiden was now within her sights. And maybe the publishers would hold back the press date, and maybe she would trot up by six lengths, and maybe...

In the event it is just as well we did not wait for Transcript. She ran twice more during the season, in a decent race at Newbury in June and in maiden company again at Haydock in July. She was unplaced both times. But if she had let us down as a performer, her career at least had gone to show what a chancy game is owning a racehorse. Sold at the autumn sales, her bad luck dogged her to the end. She broke a leg in her box, and there was no alternative but to put her down.

COURSES AROUND THE WORLD

BRITAIN 1

THE 36 flat racecourses of Britain are such a mixed bunch that visitors from overseas, used to more uniformity among their own tracks, are often surprised. Lovers of British racing claim, however, that it is largely the variety of the courses that makes the sport so enjoyable. The tight economies of the modern world have rendered certain smaller tracks unviable in recent decades, the most recent casualties being Lanark and Stockton. Some people take a pragmatic view, arguing that British racing must inevitably become more centralized and efficient, bringing itself into line with the sport in the other major European racing countries. Others mourn the disappearance of the smaller tracks and with them the variety that is the spice of life.

▶ *Clive Brittain's great filly Pebbles lands the Champion Stakes on Newmarket's Rowley Mile course.*

▼ *The July course at Newmarket.*

Newmarket
Newmarket is the "headquarters" of British horse racing and also the site of Britain's premier racecourse, or, more accurately, racecourses, as Newmarket is unique in having two, the Rowley Mile Course and the July Course.

It was Charles II who first established Newmarket as a centre for racing, and who instituted the historic race for the Town Plate. His favourite hack was Rowley, and he himself was known as "Old Rowley". The course named after him is widely regarded as being one of the best tests of the Thoroughbred in the world. Two and a quarter miles in length, the start for most races is well out of view from the stands, towards which the horses hurtle out of the vast expanse of Newmarket Heath. The straight is $1\frac{1}{4}$ miles long and fairly level until 2 furlongs out, when the horses descend from "the Bushes" into "The Dip", from which, in the final furlong, they have to extricate themselves in a stiff, testing uphill finish.

The first two Classics of the season, the 1,000 and the 2,000 Guineas, are run

on the Rowley Mile. Other famous races are the Cheveley Park, Middle Park and Dewhurst Stakes, all for two-year-olds, the Champion Stakes over 10 furlongs towards the end of the season, and the two ancient and fascinating handicaps, the Cambridgeshire and the Cesarewitch, known throughout racing as the "Autumn Double".

The July Course is used in the summer months. It shares the first part of its length, the Beacon Course, with its sister course, but it turns right into its own straight, the Bunbury Mile, which drops increasingly after ¼ mile until an uphill last furlong. The most important events are staged during the celebrated three-day July Meeting, and include high-class races such as the July Cup, the Princess of Wales' Stakes, the July Stakes and the Bunbury Cup. The July Course has its own stands and facilities.

Despite the poor viewing afforded by Newmarket, racing on either course is an experience not to be missed by any serious racegoer as there is an intensity of atmosphere that can be matched nowhere else.

Ascot

Despite serious challenges in recent years from far richer meetings like the Breeders Cup Series in the United States and the Arc de Triomphe meeting at Longchamp, Ascot's Royal meeting in June still has claims to be the best four days' racing in the world, as well as being one of the foremost events in the English social season. Highlights are the St. James' Palace Stakes, the King Edward VII Stakes, the Coronation Stakes, the King's Stand Stakes, the Ribblesdale Stakes, the Hardwicke Stakes, several important races for two-year-olds, the two great handicaps, the Royal Hunt Cup and the Wokingham, and, of course, the enthralling but sadly unfashionable Gold Cup.

In July, Ascot stages the King George and Queen Elizabeth Stakes, second only to the Prix de L'Arc de Triomphe among Europe's races for all ages, and it has recently introduced the Festival of British Racing, with the Queen Elizabeth II Stakes as the centrepiece, at the end of September.

The first meeting at Ascot was held by Queen Anne in August 1711, and the course is still owned by the monarch. The amenities and facilities offered to the racegoer are not capped by any other British racecourse, though British racecourses as a whole are not renowned for their comfort. The paddock is justly famous for its beauty.

The circuit is just over 1¾ miles long, right-handed, and triangular in shape. From the 1½-mile start it descends to Swinley Bottom and then rises all the way to the level last ½-furlong. There are two courses of 1 mile, the Old Mile,

▲
The Royal Party make their way down the course before the first at Royal Ascot.

ASCOT HATS

Many regular racegoers decide to give a miss to what is undoubtedly the best meeting of the year, Royal Ascot. Their boycott is due mainly to their intolerance of crowds of absurdly dressed people seemingly oblivious to the wonderful racing on offer and able only to talk about themselves. What is more, their ridiculous hats get in the way in paddock, bar and stands. Instead the racing aficionado stays at home and watches on television.

starting on a spur off the main course, and the straight Hunt Cup course, which goes downhill to begin with, ascends to the 5-furlong marker and then falls again until it meets the main course. The run-in is less than 3 furlongs, and the course as a whole is a testing search, well-suited to the tough, galloping type.

▼

A long distance contest at Royal Ascot.

BRITAIN 2

York

In the opinion of many people, including that of Lester Piggott, York is the best and fairest racecourse in Britain. It is set on the Knavesmire, a piece of common land where racing has been staged since 1731 and where, as its name suggests, the going can become testing after too much rain.

This left-handed circuit is shaped like a U and is 2 miles in length. Wide and flat, it affords few excuses for beaten horses, though it is especially suitable for battling, galloping types. There is a dog-legged 7 furlong course and a perfectly straight 6 furlong one. The run-in is slightly less than 5 furlongs.

The Dante meeting in May features two important Classic trials, the Dante and Musidora Stakes, as well as the famous Yorkshire Cup, while the Ebor meeting in mid-August is, after Royal Ascot, arguably the best race-meeting of the British year. Two Group One races, the Yorkshire Oaks and the International Stakes, are staged on the opening Tuesday, and other great races on the Wednesday and Thursday include the Ebor Handicap, the Great Voltigeur Stakes, the Gimcrack Stakes and the Nunthorpe Stakes.

▼
York: one of the fairest and most popular courses in Britain.

▼▼
Looking down the straight at Epsom, one of the most eccentric but exciting racetracks in the world.

Epsom

Despite other races and other meetings staged at this course on the Surrey Downs, to the world and his wife Epsom means the Derby. Instigated in 1780, it took only a few years to establish itself as the foremost race of the year, beginning to attract huge crowds in the 19th century when Derby Day was declared a national holiday, and reaching a peak in the inter-war years when an enormous attendance of half a million people became the norm.

The course itself is idiosyncratic and might even be used for a model of how not to build a racetrack in the modern age, and it is hard to think of a more vivid contrast to one of the flat, oval dirt tracks of the United States. Despite its singularity, however, the Epsom Derby course is still considered by many to be the supreme test of the middle-distance Thoroughbred, calling for speed, stamina, perfect action and a temperament that can cope with the exuberance and tension of Derby Day. It rises for the first ½ mile, bending gradually to the right, then levels off before the left-handed plunge into Tattenham Corner and the 4-furlong, cambered run-in, which ends in a stiff rise from the furlong pole. The straight 5-furlong dash is the fastest in the world.

Apart from the Derby meeting, which also includes the Coronation Cup and the Oaks, the season's fourth Classic, Epsom hosts only two other meetings a season and both of these have been in serious decline for years.

Goodwood

Goodwood's management would not take kindly to their "Glorious Goodwood" July meeting being relegated to below York's Dante meeting, as it still offers five of the best days' racing in the calendar. The main events are the Stewards Cup, the Richmond Stakes, the very prestigious and always thrilling Sussex Stakes, the Goodwood Cup and the Nassau Stakes. Other good meetings are in May and August, the latter featuring the Waterford Crystal Mile.

Goodwood is undoubtedly one of the most beautiful racecourses in the world, set up on Sussex's South Downs amid wonderful, unspoilt countryside, part of the estate of the Duke of Richmond and Gordon. The track is complicated, and is mainly right-handed, though horses competing in long distance races also have to negotiate a left-hander. There are also two points of re-entry into the straight, the longer distance races using the top bend (or one further from the stands), the 1 mile 7 furlong races the lower bend. The 1¼-mile quarter course runs in the reverse direction to the long distance races. The first 200 yards of the 6 furlong course runs uphill and then undulates mainly downhill from the 5-furlong marker. The turns and often descending gradients of Goodwood favour handy, medium-sized types over out-and-out gallopers.

▲
Glorious Goodwood.

▼
Fighting it out for the Lincoln Handicap at Doncaster.

Doncaster

Doncaster is the home of the fifth, final, oldest and least fashionable Classic race, the St. Leger, first run in 1776, while the Doncaster Cup, dating from 1766, is the oldest race in the calendar. But just as the fortunes of the St. Leger and the Cup have declined in recent years, so has the status of Doncaster itself, though, apart from some drainage problems and a severe bias in favour of well-drawn horses when the ground is soft, there is no good reason for this to be so. Until recently, it was tempting to blame an unenterprising executive (the course, also known as the Town Moor, is owned by the City Council).

Pear-shaped, left-handed, and just under 2 miles in circumference, Doncaster is a wide, fair, flat course with a run-in of almost 5 furlongs, that favours the long-striding galloper and stayer. There are both round and straight courses of 1 mile, the straight being that used for the Lincoln Handicap, the first leg of the "Spring Double" (the second leg being the Grand National).

Racing at Doncaster traditionally begins and ends the season. The highlight of the season is the St. Leger meeting in September when other good races include the Park Hill Stakes, the Champagne Stakes, the Portland Handicap and the Flying Childers Stakes. A second good meeting in October includes the Racing Post Trophy, currently the richest race for two-year-olds in the United Kingdom.

AMERICA 1

Arlington, Chicago, USA

The Arlington Million, first run over 1¼ miles in 1981, helped to prop up the ailing status of Arlington, an 11-furlong dirt track, oval and left-handed, with two inner turf courses of 1 mile and 7 furlongs. The fact that the Arlington Million is, unusually for the States, run on turf rather than dirt has accounted for its being won by several British- and French-based raiders, giving a truly international flavour to the race.

Belmont, New York, USA

The third leg of the American Triple Crown, the Belmont Stakes, is run at Belmont over 1½ miles in June, and the course also stages the Triple Crown for fillies – the Acorn Stakes (1 mile/1,600 metres), the Mother Goose Stakes (9 furlongs/1,800 metres) and the Coaching Club American Oaks (1½ miles/2,400 metres) – and the handicap Triple Crown. It is thus one of the most important tracks in the United States.

It is also one of the largest, the dirt track having a circumference of 1½ miles and a chute for a 10-furlong start. There are two inner turf tracks of 1 mile 3 furlongs and 1 mile 2 furlongs, the larger of the two having chutes for 10-furlong and 1 mile starts.

Hollywood Park, California, USA

The 1 mile dirt track at Hollywood Park is the normal left-handed oval with various chutes for different starts, but the inner turf track of 7 furlongs allows a slight variation, having a spur across the middle of the course for a 9-furlong gate. The turf track is best known for its two great races, the Hollywood Invitational Turf Handicap and the Turf Cup, while the Hollywood Gold Cup Handicap is run on the dirt. The glamorous, sophisticated and luxurious Hollywood Park was also the choice to host the first ever Breeders Cup Series.

Laurel, Maryland, USA

The Washington DC International was the first race anywhere in the world to be specifically designed for an international field, entries being by invitation only. The first running, in 1952, fielded runners from five countries and was won by

▶
Chief's Crown wins the dirt race for the Breeders Cup at Hollywood Park in 1984.

▼
Racing at Belmont Park and Arlington (inset).

a British horse, and the race has retained a genuinely international character ever since, with France providing by far the most successful of the foreign raiders over the years.

In 1985 the race was cut in distance to 1¼ miles (and is currently sponsored by Budweiser), and an improvement in both the supporting card and the racecourse's facilities have ensured that a decline in the race's fortunes has now been halted. Both the dirt and turf tracks are left-handed ovals of 1 mile in circumference, the former having separate chutes for 7-furlong, 1-mile and 10½ -furlong starts.

Pimlico, Maryland, USA

Pimlico is home to the second and shortest race of the American Triple Crown, the Preakness Stakes, over 9½ furlongs (1,900 metres). Crowds of little less than 100,000 will be attracted to the course on that third Saturday in May, but otherwise attendances are more like one-tenth of that figure, and Pimlico has to some extent to live in the shadow of other big courses in the area.

The dirt-track is a left-handed oval of 1 mile with two chutes for 6- and 10-furlong races. There is an inner turf track of 7 furlongs.

AMERICA 2

Santa Anita, California, USA

Santa Anita is an excellent and justly popular track just outside Los Angeles. The left-handed oval dirt track is 1 mile in circumference with chutes for 7- and 10-furlong starts. There is also a turf course that seems almost to be European; it begins some way outside the rest of the track, 10 furlongs away from the winning post, and allows races of up to 14 furlongs to be run in conjunction with the main course.

Great prizes at the course include the Santa Anita Handicap, the Santa Anita Derby, the San Juan Capistrano Handicap (at 1¾ miles/2,800 metres, the longest Grade One event in the United States), the Charles H. Shrub Stakes, the Santa Margarita Invitational Handicap, the Yellow Ribbon Stakes and the Oak Tree Invitational Stakes.

▼ *Contesting the Breeders Cup at Santa Anita in 1986.*

Churchill Downs, Kentucky, USA

One hundred and fifty thousand people crowd into Churchill Downs on the first Saturday of each May to witness the first leg in the American Triple Crown, the Kentucky Derby, run over 1¼ miles (2,000 metres). They are there not only to watch one of the most famous and prestigious horse races in the world, but also to sample the comforts and luxuries of this extremely well-appointed track that can boast average crowds of 20,000 despite, apart from Kentucky Derby day, the comparative modesty of the racing on offer.

As with all racecourses in the USA, the track is a flat, left-handed oval. The dirt track is 1 mile in circumference with a chute off the far bend opposite the stands providing an almost straight mile. Inside the dirt oval there is a slightly smaller (7 furlongs) turf oval created when Churchill Downs hosted the Breeders Cup series in 1988.

Woodbine, Toronto, Canada

The new Woodbine course, built in 1956, is an especially pleasant racetrack, combining as it does the best of North American and European racing styles. The course itself reflects this. There are the usual left-handed, oval dirt and turf tracks with their various chutes, but there is also an extra turf course beginning outside the main arena, 10 furlongs from the post, and allowing a larger variation of distances than usual.

Among the great races run at the Woodbine track are the Queen's Plate Stakes, the Rothmans International Stakes and the E.P. Taylor Stakes.

San Isidro, Buenos Aires, Argentina

Both the Gran Premio Club (the Argentinian Derby) and the Gran Premio Carlos Pellegrini (the fourth leg of a Quadruple Crown unique to Argentina) are run at San Isidro, a few miles north of Buenos Aires, and the most important course in the whole of the South American continent. Almost 2 miles in circumference, this turf track has a straight 5 furlongs and another long spur off to the north giving a dog-leg of 7 furlongs, but its similarities to European tracks end there. The styles of riding, training on the course and the strange alliance of incredibly busy and tight schedules with a totally relaxed approach proclaim San Isidro to be firmly in the southern hemisphere.

▶
The grandstand at Churchill Downs.

▼
Coming out of the stalls at Santa Anita in 1986.

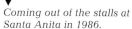

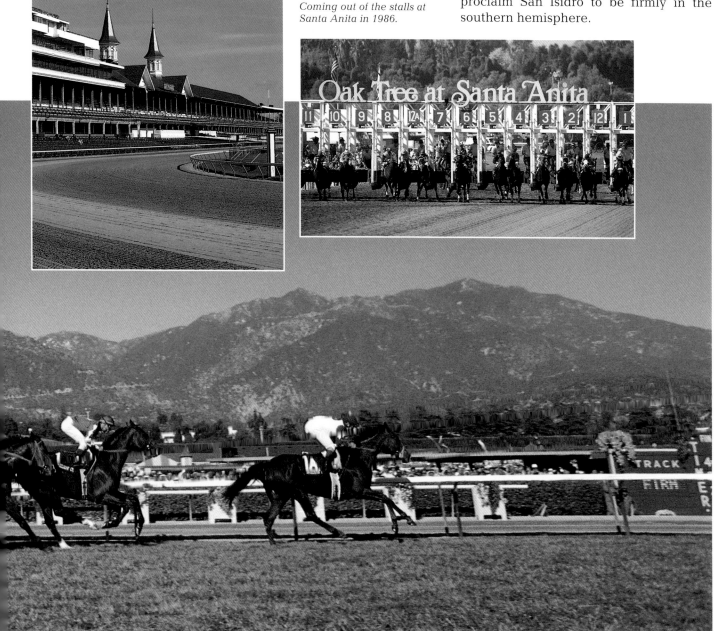

EUROPE 1

Chantilly, France

The area of Chantilly is, like Newmarket in England, the main training ground for the French-trained racehorse, though its delightful surroundings of woods and lakes could hardly be less like the windswept Suffolk heath. Chantilly race-course, for no very good reason, is only frequented during the month of June, when the Prix du Jockey Club (the French Derby) and the Prix de Diane (the French Oaks), two of the most important events in the calendar, are held there, and many believe that the attractive, atmospheric and fair course, a sharp, testing righthander with an abnormally long straight, should be used more often, though at present a crowd of more than a few thousand racegoers begins, in fact, to strain the facilities.

The Curragh, Republic of Ireland

The Curragh was always the emerald among Irish racecourses, and with the recent demise of Phoenix Park, it now stands alone and unrivalled. There has always been racing on the great plain of the Curragh, and it has for many years also been the main training centre of Ireland, playing a role that is similar to Newmarket's in England. All five Irish Classics, among many other important races, are staged at the course, a horse-shoe-shaped 2 mile circuit with easy bends and a straight of 3 furlongs with an uphill finish, all going to favour the long-striding horse with good stamina.

Leopardstown is another good Irish track, modelled on Sandown Park and boasting almost as good facilities as its English cousin, and though it is particularly well-known for its jumping, it also stages five Group races on the flat.

▲
Grand surroundings at Chantilly, France.

◀
Hats and high fashion at Chantilly, France.

◀◀
Keeping traditions alive at Chantilly, France.

◀
Competing for the Irish Oaks at the Curragh, in the Irish Republic.

Baden-Baden, Germany

Baden-Baden is a delightful and popular track which stages two main meetings a year, in the spring and the autumn, culminating on the final Sunday of the season with the running of the Grosser Preis von Baden over 1½ miles (2,400 metres). Both festivals attract large crowds who revel in the holiday atmosphere and make full use of the excellent facilities. Many people arrive fairly early at the course in order to have breakfast while watching the horses out an exercise.

The track itself is a tight left-handed circuit of nearly 1¼ miles (2,000 metres) with a 3-furlong run in and an eccentric 6-furlong course that is straight except for a dog-leg 300 yards from the finish, which can cause some problems.

Other important tracks in Germany include Cologne, the centre of German racing and home of the country's most valuable race, the Puma-Europa-Preis and the Mehl-Mulhens-Rennen (the German 2,000 Guineas); and Hamburg, which may not be everybody's favourite racecourse but is home of the Deutsches Derby, the Grosser Hansa-Preis and the Sprinter-Preis.

EUROPE 2

Longchamp, France

Set in the Bois de Boulogne just to the west of Paris, and home of the Prix de L'Arc de Triomphe, Longchamp is France's number one racecourse. It holds centre stage on every Sunday (France's main racing day) throughout April and May, during which time it puts on the Prix d'Essai des Poulains and the Prix d'Essai des Pouliches (the French 1,000 and 2,000 Guineas), and the main trials for the Prix du Jockey Club and the Prix de Diane (the French Derby and Oaks both run at Chantilly in June).

In June there is the Grand Prix de Paris meeting, and then Longchamp takes a rest until returning in September for a top-class, eight-day meeting of races of the calibre of the Prix du Moulin, the Prix Vermeille, the Prix du Salamandre, the Grand Criterium, the Prix de la Forêt and the final French Classic, the Prix Royal Oak.

Yet surpassing all that has gone before is the Arc meeting held on the first weekend in October. The Arc has now become established as the unofficial all-aged, middle-distance championship of Europe, and its supporting races, like the Prix Marcel Boussac and the Prix de l'Abbaye de Longchamp, in no way let it down. On this weekend a vast invasion of Englishmen, Scotsmen, Welshmen and Irishmen swell the French crowds to levels comparable to Longchamp's heyday in the first quarter of the 20th century.

The course itself has three separate right-handed turns at one end, for races of different distances, the furthest producing an overall circumference of 1¾ miles. There is also a straight 5 furlong course across the far side of the course. Facilities are excellent, and Longchamp in general exudes a certain chic, expected from the course that is the first choice of Parisian and French racegoers.

The other principal French tracks on the Parisian circuit are Chantilly, Saint-Cloud, Maisons-Laffitte, Evry, and, the odd-man-out, Deauville on the Norman coast, to which the entire French circus decamps during the long and sultry month of August.

◀ *Dwarfed by the windmill at Longchamp, France.*

▲ *The paddock at Longchamp, France.*

DEAUVILLE

In August the French racing community decamps to the Norman seaside town of Deauville, where the seventeen days of racing includes two Group One contests, Le Prix Jacques Le Marois for three-year olds and up over a mile, won in 1987 and 1988 by the great filly Miesque, and Le Prix Morny for two-year olds. The track is an exciting one, and the short 2½ furlong run-in benefits horses that can come with a late run.

Despite pleas that the annual sojourn in Deauville is neither efficient or cost-effective, it is very much an established part of the French racing calendar, particularly as it is accompanied by the most

important yearling sales in France. Normandy is, after all, home to the best studs in the country. Meanwhile the town prospers on the annual influx of people, the horses benefit from the sea air and their morning exercise on the beach, and at night the cards click and the roulette wheels rattle in the casinos.

San Siro, Italy

In the great days of the Tesio de Montel rivalry in the 1920s and 1930s, San Siro, the racecourse of Milan, was one of the most exciting tracks in the world. It still has an atmosphere of exhilaration that is completely lacking at its Roman counterpart, Capannelle, despite the fact that the latter stages the Derby Italiano, the Premio Parioli (the Italian 2,000 Guineas) and the Premio Regina Elena (the Italian 1,000 Guineas), and despite the fact, too, that Italian racing has been in decline for some years and that its top races are very often won by foreign-trained horses.

Major races run at San Siro include the Classic Oaks d'Italia, the Gran Premio di Milano, the Gran Premio d'Italia, the Gran Premio del Jockey Club and the Gran Criterium. The sophisticated layout of the track allows for many variations of race. Just under 2 miles (3,200 metres) in circumference at best, San Siro is a broad, right-handed, galloping track which lays an emphasis on stamina, particularly with its searching uphill straight of 4½ furlongs (900 metres).

REST OF THE WORLD

Flemington, Victoria, Australia

The Melbourne Cup is one of those races, like the Epsom and Kentucky Derbys, which has become world famous in its own right, but it does not really deserve its position of eminence in the eyes of the purist. For the Melbourne Cup is only a handicap, albeit an extremely well-endowed handicap, and is run over the extreme distance of 2 miles. Yet on the first Tuesday of November the entire state of Victoria moves into party gear, and some 100,000 people converge on Flemington racecourse.

A splendid, left-handed, pear-shaped turf track of 11½ furlongs, favouring the long-striding type of horse, Flemington has a 6-furlong straight, halfway down which the Melbourne Cup is started. Other great races run at the course include the Victoria Derby, the L.K.S. McKinnon Stakes, the V.R.C. Oaks, the Ampol Stakes, the Queen Elizabeth Stakes, the Australian Cup and the Newmarket Handicap.

▼ *The pear-shaped track at Flemington, Australia.*

Vying with Flemington for superiority in Australia is Randwick, Sydney's number one course and home not only to the Australian Jockey Club Derby, Oaks and St. Leger but also, in typical Australian style, such popular events as the Sydney Cup, the Epsom Handicap and the Metropolitan Handicap, over 13 furlongs. Other fine racecourses in Australia include Ascot, Brisbane, Moonee Valley, Morphettville and Rosehill.

Fuchu, Tokyo, Japan

The Japan Cup, over 11 miles, is the most valuable race in the world and very much the highlight of the Japanese racing year. Run in November, the best horses from the rest of the world are invited to take part and quite often win it. The 11-furlong, oval, turf course can often ride firm and an uphill section towards the stands brings stamina into play in long-distance races. It encloses a dirt track of 10 furlongs. Huge crowds swarm to the course at weekends, and on big occasions the numbers can top the 150,000 mark.

Sha Tin, Hong Kong

Despite the mediocrity of the horses, racing at Sha Tin is an experience that should not be missed. The vast, gambling-mad crowds and the superb facilities make for a day out that cannot be surpassed in terms of excitement by many other courses. Sha Tin was built on land reclaimed from the sea and held its first meeting on 7th October 1978. The right-handed turf course (the turf is laid into a special sand and wire base to help drainage) is an oval of 10 furlongs, with chutes for 5- and 9-furlong starts, enclosing a similarly shaped dirt track.

There is also stabling for 1,000 horses. Among the big races, or betting mediums, of the year are the Sha Tin Trophy, the Hong Kong Derby and the Hong Kong Invitation Cup. Sha Tin has taken the pressure of Hong Kong's other and older racecourse, Happy Valley, in the centre of the island, where space is so limited that the horses are stabled in tower blocks and exercised on the roofs, but where some highly entertaining racing is still staged.

▲
Heading for victory in the Invitation Cup at Sha Tin in 1990.

▼
A big day out at Flemington, Australia.

Trentham, Wellington, New Zealand

New Zealand's importance as a breeding country rather outweighs its racing, but Trentham, an undulating, left-handed, oval, grass course of nearly 10 furlongs (2,000 metres) stages a clutch of excellent races, such as the New Zealand Oaks and St. Leger, the Wellington Cup and the Trentham Stakes.

Other good racecourses in the country include Te Rapa, Ellerslie and Riccarton.

THE FUTURE OF HORSERACING

Britain

As this book went to press, the future of British racing looked as uncertain as at any time in its long history. The very future of the Jockey Club itself seemed in doubt. The parliamentary Home Affairs Select Committee on Horseracing had just published its report and its findings had on the whole made a great deal of sense.

If, as seemed likely, the Home Secretary was to implement its recommendations, radical changes would sweep across British racing. The Jockey Club, Levy Board and Horseracing Advisory council were likely to be amalgamated into a single controlling authority, while the bookmakers would at last be forced to put more money back into the industry. Betting shops would be allowed to open until 9 in the evening, to take advantage of evening racing, while Sunday racing would be introduced. Meanwhile, the continuing recession meant that some 300 fixtures were likely to be dropped from the calendar, and the future of various racecourses looked less than rosy.

Though British racing has arguably been best in the world for the last decade, it is no doubt currently in a state of crisis, and the smaller breeders, owners, trainers and racecourses are being forced out of business. The single main problem is the ridiculously low level of prize money, especially at the bottom end of the game, and this in turn has been caused by the long-term failure of the authorities to make the bookmakers put back a sufficient amount of money into the sport.

The World

World horseracing, on the other hand, is full of exciting developments, best of all its increasing internationalism, a process which seems likely to accelerate in the future. It is now possible to foresee a time when horses from different continents will be taking each other on as a matter of course, and when an international world classification system will be embarked upon.

As styles of racing and racecourses differ around the world, the question is which will become dominant, and this is not easy to answer. The methods of the all-powerful USA will be likely to prevail, as they do in so many areas of modern life, but it is to be hoped that some of the legacy that Europe, and England in particular, has given the world, especially in the art of training and in the variety of racecourses, will not be completely overshadowed.

Above all there is the hope that it is now only a matter of time before the best trainers, jockeys and horses from all over the world will be travelling from course to course and from country to country, battling it out in front of the stands for our continued delight for only one simple reason – to see which horse is the fastest.

▲
Dirt racing at Churchill Downs, Kentucky. European horses will have to compete on surfaces like this in their bid to take some of the big American prizes in the future.

GLOSSARY

AGED A term to describe any horse over six years old.

ALL OUT A term to describe a horse under maximum pressure during a race.

ALL-WEATHER GALLOP A training strip of artificial surface.

ANTE-POST Betting before the day of a race.

COLT An entire male thoroughbred of less than five years old.

COME WITH A WET SAIL, TO To make rapid progress in a race.

CONNECTIONS All those people connected with a horse.

COVER UP A HORSE, TO To keep it in behind others in a race.

DISTANCE, THE About 250 yards from the winning post.

DO A HORSE, TO For a stable lad to look after a horse.

ENTIRE HORSE An uncastrated horse.

EVENING STABLES The afternoon/evening feeding and mucking out time.

FILLY A female thoroughbred of less than five years old.

FURLONG 220 yards.

GELDING A castrated colt or horse.

GET A TRIP, TO For a horse to be effective over long distances.

HACK A horse used by his trainer to ride out with his string.

HEADQUARTERS Newmarket.

HORSE An entire male thoroughbred of five years old or more.

LIE HANDY, TO To be handily placed in a race.

LISTED RACE A race just below Group status.

LOT A batch of horses ready for exercise.

MARE A female thoroughbred of five years or more.

MONKEY £500 in betting parlance.

NON-TRIER A horse which is not trying its best in a race.

OVERNIGHTS The final list of horses declared to run at the next day's race meetings.

PONY £25 in betting parlance.

PULLS OUT A lot leaves, or "pulls out", of the yard for exercise.

RACING MANAGER A manager of an owner's horses.

RIDE WORK, TO To ride a horse out at exercise.

SEE DAYLIGHT, TO To see a gap appear between horses racing ahead.

SENIOR STEWARD Temporary principal, effectively chairman, of Jockey Club.

STICK, THE The whip.

STRING Inmates of a stable – "Clive Brittain's string".

STRIP FITTER, TO To appear fitter than last time.

TATTERSALLS The biggest, medium-priced, enclosure on a racecourse.

TROT UP, TO To win a race very easily.

UPSIDES Horses racing alongside each other.

WASTE, TO For a jockey to shed weight by various means.

INDEX

page numbers in italic refer to photographs

ACKNOWLEDGEMENTS

Trevor Jones: pp. 1, 3, 6/7, 8/9, 10/11, 12/13, 14/15, 16/17, 18/19, 20 (bottom), 22/23, 25, 26, 27, 32/33, 34/35, 36/37, 38/39, 40/41, 42/43, 44/45, 46/47, 48/49, 50/51, 52/53, 54/55, 56/57, 58/59, 60/61, 62/63, 64/65, 66/67, 68/69, 70/71, 72/73, 74/75, 76/77, 78/79, 80/81, 81, 82/83, 84/85, 86, 87 (top), 88, 90/91, 92 (left and top), 93 (top), 94/95, 96/97, 98/99, 100, 102/103, 104/105, 106/107, 108/109, 110/111, 112, 112/113 (across bottom), 113 (top), 114/115, 116/117, 118/119, 120/121, 122/123, 124/125, 126 (inset), 126/127 (across bottom), 129 (left), 130/131, 132, 133 (top), 136/137.

George Selwyn: 20 (top), 21, 24/25 (across top), 26/27 (bottom), 80 (top), 89, 92 (bottom), 93 (bottom), 101 (top and bottom), 113 (bottom), 127, 128/129 (across bottom), 129 (right), 133 (bottom), 134/135.

E.T. Archive: 28/29.

S & G Press Agency: 30/31.

Technical Racing Services: 87 (bottom).

FOR MORGAN SAMUEL EDITIONS

Managing Editor: Pip Morgan
Editorial: Helen Douglas-Cooper, Peter Price, Rob Saunders, Susanne Haines
Editorial Assistant: Nisha Jani
Index: Simone Lefolii
Design: Trevor Spooner and Blackjacks
Publisher: Nigel Perryman

Morgan Samuel Editions would particlarly like to thank Clive Brittain and the staff of the Carlburg Stables, Newmarket, for their generous help during the production of this book.